True Crime Trivia & Activity Book

T0395468

ALSO BY LANA BARNES

Logic Puzzles Book for Brain Fitness

TRUE CRIME

Trivia & Activity Book

Untangle the Secrets Behind History's Most Gripping Crimes

T0395988

ZEITGEIST • NEW YORK

Copyright © 2024 by Penguin Random House LLC

All rights reserved.
Published in the United States by Zeitgeist™, an imprint and
division of Penguin Random House LLC, New York.
zeitgeistpublishing.com

Zeitgeist™ is a trademark of Penguin Random House LLC.
ISBN: 9780593689868

Cover art © by DONOT6_STUDIO, Natasha Barsova,
Mark Carrel, Mauro Rodrigues/Shutterstock.com
Illustrations by Matthew Hollings
Collages by Emma Hall
Collage art © by Claudio Divizia/Shutterstock.com [page 15], Digital Storm/Shutterstock.com [page 26], Popup, Rroselavy, New Africa/Shutterstock.com [page 41], *Fruit and Vegetable Market with a Young Fruit Seller* (1650–1660) by Jan van Kessel, *Butterfly, Caterpillar, Moth, Insects, and Currants* (1650–1655) by Jan van Kessel, *Insects, Butterflies, and a Grasshopper* (1664), *Vanitas Still Life* (ca.1665–1670) by Jan van Kessel [page 43], shurkin_son, Moloko88, Vector Tradition, Fortis Design, David Smart, singkam, HD92, Aleksey Belorukov, Fenixx666, SaveJungle/Shutterstock.com [page 53], Fer Gregory, Jarhe Photography, felipe caparros, Gorodenkoff, New Africa/Shutterstock.com [page 57], Alila Medical Media/Shutterstock.com [page 73], Gorodenkoff/Shutterstock.com [page 81], nadi555, AlexLMX, Photoongraphy, S-Studio, Oleksii Arseniuk, New Africa, Dmitr1ch, Forgotron/Shutterstock.com [page 92], baldezh/Shutterstock.com [page 101], Nosyrevy, adwar/Shutterstock.com [page 117], Kevin L Chesson, Shawn Hempel, Brandon Alms, Sergei Drozd/Shutterstock.com [page 135], Miloje, Mind Pixell, Wstockstudio/Shutterstock.com [page 142]
Book design by Aimee Fleck
Author photograph © by Asher Hung
Edited by Ada Fung

Printed in the United States of America
1st Printing

Introduction

Welcome, fellow true crime aficionados! My name is Lana Barnes, and I have a confession: I am true crime obsessed. There's just something so satisfying about gathering clues and forming conclusions about how or why something happened, and I want to share that satisfaction with other people just as fascinated with true crime as I am. What better way than with an activity book dedicated to the subject?

I've curated a mix of crime types as puzzle themes, including art heists, catfishing, forgeries, fraud, cults, and abductions, just to name a few. These crimes are from varying historical eras and include crimes from all over the world!

Some of the puzzles are meant to test and improve your memory, logic, reasoning, and deductive skills—skills that crime investigators use to solve crimes. In this book, you'll find word-based activities (e.g., crosswords, acrostics, logic grid puzzles), number-based activities (e.g., sudoku, kakuro), and visual-based activities (e.g., spot the difference, find the match). Trivia is also sprinkled throughout to test your knowledge about real crimes and criminal investigation processes. All the trivia and facts in the book are verified to the best of my ability, but since I've included some cold cases, some of the information might be disputed or disproven later.

I know better than anyone how strange it might be to pair true crime with puzzles (telling my husband he's on his own while I "solve crimes" has gotten me an odd look here and there!), but I also know that both serve similar purposes for me and others like me—both can be a way to unwind and stimulate the mind. I fully realize that the cases I mention involve real people. In putting this puzzle book together, I've aimed to be as respectful and considerate as possible of the people involved in the crimes and of you, the puzzler! And it goes without saying that I do not in any way condone the criminal activity that is discussed in this book. Now, let's get to it!

Puzzle Instructions

How to Solve Crosswords

The first step in solving a crossword puzzle is to scan all the clues and mark the ones you feel most confident about. Look for clues that you know definite answers for and start with shorter words—these are a quick way to fill the grid and set up jumping-off points for harder clues.

Once you've filled in the words you definitely know, move on to some of the trickier clues. Look at words that cross other words to help solve these. Use the number of letters in the word and any letters you've already filled in to narrow down potential answers.

Sometimes clues can be misleading. You'll need to think outside the box for these and consider alternative meanings or synonyms. The way the clue is phrased can sometimes also help. If you get stuck, take a break or move on. Sometimes, solving other clues can help unlock trouble areas.

How to Solve Sudoku

Sudoku is a number-based logic game that doesn't require arithmetic. A sudoku puzzle is made up of a 9x9 grid of squares divided into nine 3x3 square blocks. Some of the squares are already filled in with numbers, and you must fill in the remaining squares so that each of the numbers 1 through 9 appears exactly once in each row, column, and block.

Start with the rows, columns, and blocks that have the most numbers filled in. These partially filled-in sections will help quickly eliminate possibilities for each square. Once those are filled in, use "cross-hatching" to fill in the rest. Look at where a number is in other columns, rows, and blocks to find which columns, rows, and blocks the number can't appear in again.

If you've exhausted all possibilities through cross-hatching but still have some empty squares, try writing down two or three possible answers for each square.

How to Solve Cryptograms

Cryptograms are coded messages where each letter in the original text has been replaced by a number. Start by analyzing how many times a letter appears in the encoded message. In the English language, the letters E, T, and A occur more frequently than others. Look for common patterns or repeated numbers in the encoded text that could represent these frequently used letters.

Next, use clues or patterns within the passage. Short words or common phrases, like "the" or "and," might offer clues to frequently used letters, which can then help you decode the rest of the message. If there are single-letter words, you can bet they're probably A or I.

Using the letters and patterns you've identified, use trial and error to try out possible letters in the coded message. Logical deduction (as well as persistence!) is key in solving these puzzles.

How to Solve Acrostics

Acrostic puzzles are a mix of crossword puzzles and cryptograms. To solve an acrostic puzzle, you must fill in the grid with the answers to the given clues. The initial letters of each line in the puzzle will reveal a hidden word or phrase—the solution to the acrostic! Begin by reading through the clues carefully, focusing on the easiest ones first. Once you've gotten all the answers you're sure about out of the way, move on to the trickier clues. If you are stuck on a clue, try using possible letter patterns in the revealed word to figure out what letter an unknown clue's answer might start with.

These layered puzzles can be difficult, but with a little bit of patience and perseverance, you'll figure them out!

How to Solve Logic Grid Puzzles

Each logic grid puzzle has a scenario and an objective. The scenario gives you clues, which you record in a grid. In the grid are categories and items in those categories. Each item matches with another item in a different category; no two items in a category can be a match with the same item in another category. Using the clues given and logical deduction, you must find each item's unique match.

First, read the information at the beginning of the puzzle and familiarize yourself with the different categories and items in the grid and your objective. Next, read the clues and record the information you find in the grid. Draw a circle for items that match and an X for items that don't match. Once you've filled in the grid, double-check that all the info you've recorded is accurate. After you've recorded the given information, you'll need to use deduction to uncover the rest of the matches. Read clues carefully and be on the lookout for information you may have overlooked.

How to Solve Futoshiki

A futoshiki puzzle is made up of a 4x4 grid of squares with inequality symbols (<, or less than, and >, or greater than) between some of the squares. There will be some squares already filled in with numbers. You must fill in the rest of the squares so that each of the numbers 1 through 4 appears exactly once in each row and column and the relationships between the squares meet the constraints of the inequality symbols.

First, identify squares that can have only one answer based on the inequality symbols and surrounding squares. Add these definite numbers to the grid. Then look for rows or columns with the fewest possibilities based on the given inequality symbols. Use the inequalities to figure out relationships between adjacent squares. If a square is greater than another square in the same row or column, eliminate numbers that are impossible based on this relationship.

How to Solve Kakuro

Kakuro puzzles are like crossword puzzles, but instead of words, you use numbers to solve the puzzle. Each blank square in the grid must contain the numbers 1 through 9 in such a way that the numbers you fill in add up to the given clues in the black, prefilled squares. Clues will be on the right for blank squares that run across and on the top for blank squares that run down. Numbers cannot repeat in any across or down "run" of numbers.

Start by identifying rows or columns with the fewest possible combinations, typically those with the largest sums or shared numbers. Look for clues that can be solved only one way. For instance, a sum of 3 across two spaces means the only possible numbers are 1 and 2. Look for opportunities where certain numbers can only fit into specific spaces. For instance, if a row with a sum of 6 has three empty spaces, the only combination is 1, 2, and 3.

How to Solve Magic Square Puzzles

A magic square puzzle is another type of number-based logic puzzle. Each puzzle is divided into squares, and the squares in each row, column, and diagonal must add up to the same sum—the magic number. This book has 3x3 and 4x4 magic squares, and the magic numbers are given in the instructions for each grid.

Hook, Line, and Sinker

Answer the questions to test your knowledge about scams.

1. True or false: The first Nigerian prince imposter was a fourteen-year-old American boy.
2. What do you call the people who expose scammers?
3. The earliest recorded attempt at insurance fraud was in 300 B.C. when Hegastratos, a Greek sea merchant, took out money against his ship and its cargo. What did he unsuccessfully try to do to avoid repaying his loan?
   a. Burned the ship and its cargo
   b. Sunk the ship
   c. Never showed up at his final destination
   d. Told authorities his ship was robbed
4. This symbol of fraud was a legitimate medicine used for centuries in China to help reduce inflammation.
5. How did mid-1800s photographer William H. Mumler trick his clients into thinking the ghostly figures that appeared behind them in his photos were their dead loved ones?
   a. He had people stand behind them when he took the photo
   b. He manipulated the photo after it was printed
   c. He produced images with double exposures
   d. He hypnotized his clients
6. What was amateur archaeologist Shinichi Fujimura caught doing at a site in Kamitakamori, Japan?
   a. Stealing artifacts so he could sell them on the black market
   b. Swapping out artifacts with fakes
   c. Doing illegal tours of the site for wealthy citizens
   d. Planting artifacts so his team could get credit for discovering the oldest stone artifacts in Japan
7. What is the animal-themed nickname for someone who launders money from victims of fraud?
8. Who catfished rapper Iggy Azalea by posing as a fan and becoming social media friends with her?
9. Who did Oscar Hartzell target in the Sir Francis Drake Estate Scam?
   a. People who had the surname Drake
   b. People who were knighted by the king
   c. People who owned land in Spain
   d. People who served in the US Navy
10. How did the electronics and appliances retail store chain Crazy Eddie commit one of the longest-running frauds in modern times?
   a. Paying employees off the books
   b. Skimming sales tax
   c. Under-reporting income
   d. All of the above

The Art of the Heist

Across

4. _______ and grab
5. This FBI unit was formed in 2004 to recover artifacts stolen from the Baghdad Museum
6. Art thief Vjeran Tomic was given this nickname for his penchant for scaling the sides of buildings in Paris to steal valuable items
9. *Poppy Flowers* by this Dutch artist has been stolen twice (two words)
11. The getaway vehicle when a Rembrandt was stolen for the second time
16. Jan van Eyck's *Ghent* _______ is the most frequently stolen artwork in history
18. Maurizio Cattelan's *America*, a fully functioning gold _______, was stolen from the Blenheim Palace
20. Bullfight call
22. *The Scream* was stolen from this city on the opening day of the Olympics
24. Polish pirates stole Flemish painter Hans Memling's *The Last Judgment* while it was traveling by ship to this Italian city
27. Yellow fruit
28. Prefix meaning not
29. Art forger Pei-Shen Qian used these to age paintings (two words)

Down

1. Steak order
2. Gallery security worker
3. Fried Hanukkah treats
4. The biggest unsolved art theft in history was from the Isabella _______ Gardner Museum
7. Documentation that proves the authenticity of an artwork
8. Robbers of the Nationalmuseum in Stockholm in 2000 threw _______ on the road to obstruct police cars
10. Paintings were stolen from the Whitworth Art Gallery in the UK supposedly to draw attention to its poor _______
12. Involving more than one
13. Separate
14. The theft of Rembrandt's _______ *Bartholomew* was part of the first-ever armed art robbery
15. _______ Picasso is the most stolen artist
17. The thieves in Canada's largest art heist entered through this
19. Sweet frozen dessert (two words)
21. Therefore
23. Art thief Stéphane Breitwieser was convinced he suffered from this syndrome
25. Calf-length trousers
26. Steal artwork for ransom

1
2
3
4
5
6
7
8
9
10
11
12
13
14
15
16
17
18
19
20
21
22
23
24
25
26
27
28
29

Chicago Tylenol Murders

Find all the listed words in the grid of letters. Words can be found in any direction—horizontally, vertically, or diagonally. They can be either forward or backward.

G	O	M	T	B	G	E	Y	S	N	A	T	F	E	M	I	T	G	A	S	N	H	Q
S	D	U	O	B	R	F	D	H	Y	C	X	R	E	K	E	Q	N	E	H	F	G	U
Q	D	R	N	J	C	G	I	M	F	Y	Z	D	D	E	T	N	I	A	T	Z	C	E
Z	E	D	I	N	A	Y	C	U	D	R	I	L	L	B	O	A	R	D	H	I	L	K
T	X	E	I	I	P	X	C	D	B	C	Z	B	A	I	E	V	E	Q	Q	U	J	T
P	T	R	I	G	B	T	J	R	A	A	J	C	Q	S	L	S	P	W	S	C	L	I
X	R	B	G	C	E	Z	Z	T	V	O	R	A	R	A	P	U	M	P	R	A	E	B
N	A	V	D	N	M	L	I	M	O	G	H	P	J	D	Z	D	A	O	C	V	D	V
E	S	E	W	C	R	O	G	E	R	A	R	N	O	L	D	C	T	E	E	D	A	D
V	T	P	A	N	N	N	V	A	I	C	W	X	G	I	W	V	D	H	Y	N	F	H
E	R	W	D	P	O	E	D	F	W	I	Q	J	V	L	L	A	C	E	R	Q	D	M
S	E	P	C	J	S	L	S	C	W	H	T	N	Y	H	U	H	R	H	C	R	D	P
C	N	H	X	P	I	Y	W	R	N	C	R	E	L	L	I	K	N	I	A	P	N	F
D	G	K	S	Z	O	T	J	R	Q	A	B	A	Y	C	O	L	D	C	A	S	E	E
X	T	Q	X	A	P	K	R	S	I	W	E	L	S	E	M	A	J	W	N	X	Z	E
X	H	E	X	T	K	Q	R	A	X	A	E	X	D	F	Q	X	T	B	N	Y	J	G

Word Bank

capsule	cyanide	James Lewis	murder	recall	tainted
Chicago	drill board	laced	painkiller	Roger Arnold	tampering
cold case	extra strength	medication	poison	seven	Tylenol

Check the Call Log

These two call logs may look the same but check again! There are 10 differences. Can you find them?

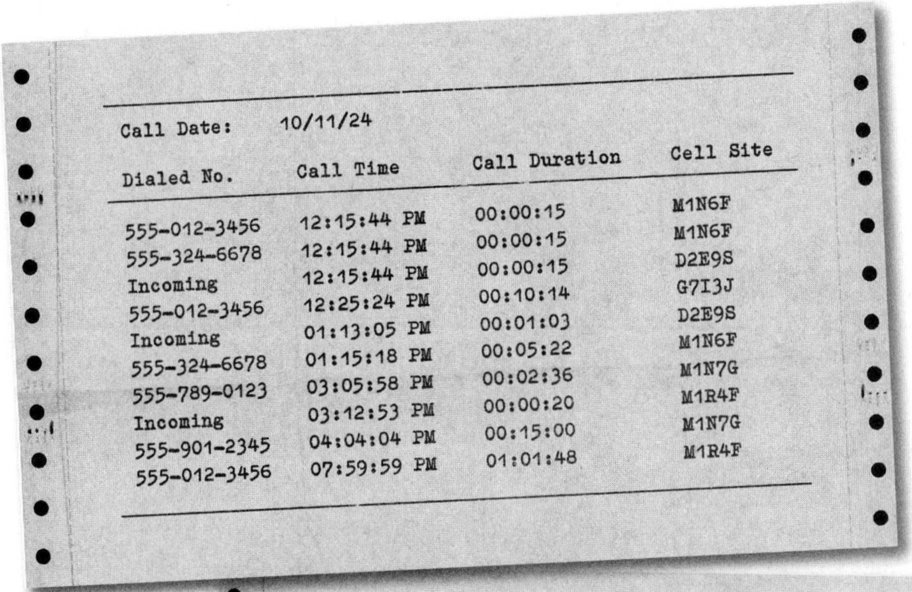

Call Date: 10/11/24

Dialed No.	Call Time	Call Duration	Cell Site
555-012-3456	12:15:44 PM	00:00:15	M1N6F
555-324-6678	12:15:44 PM	00:00:15	M1N6F
Incoming	12:15:44 PM	00:00:15	D2E9S
555-012-3456	12:25:24 PM	00:10:14	G7I3J
Incoming	01:13:05 PM	00:01:03	D2E9S
555-324-6678	01:15:18 PM	00:05:22	M1N6F
555-789-0123	03:05:58 PM	00:02:36	M1N7G
Incoming	03:12:53 PM	00:00:20	M1R4F
555-901-2345	04:04:04 PM	00:15:00	M1N7G
555-012-3456	07:59:59 PM	01:01:48	M1R4F

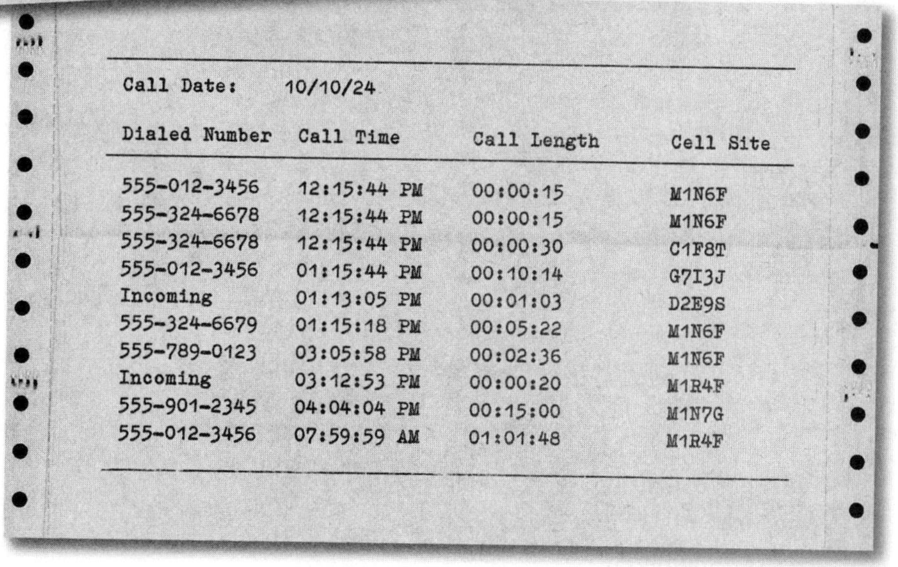

Call Date: 10/10/24

Dialed Number	Call Time	Call Length	Cell Site
555-012-3456	12:15:44 PM	00:00:15	M1N6F
555-324-6678	12:15:44 PM	00:00:15	M1N6F
555-324-6678	12:15:44 PM	00:00:30	C1F8T
555-012-3456	01:15:44 PM	00:10:14	G7I3J
Incoming	01:13:05 PM	00:01:03	D2E9S
555-324-6679	01:15:18 PM	00:05:22	M1N6F
555-789-0123	03:05:58 PM	00:02:36	M1N6F
Incoming	03:12:53 PM	00:00:20	M1R4F
555-901-2345	04:04:04 PM	00:15:00	M1N7G
555-012-3456	07:59:59 AM	01:01:48	M1R4F

Where in the World?

Answer the questions to test your knowledge about crimes that have taken place outside the United States.

1. In 2011 and 2012, a team of thieves stole 2,700 tons of ______ from a reserve maintained in Québec.
2. "The Isdal Woman," who went by many aliases, including Fenella Lorch, was found dead in a remote wooded valley in which Northern European country?
   a. Norway
   b. Sweden
   c. Finland
   d. Denmark
3. The Irish Crown Jewels were stolen in 1907 and never recovered. Which historical site were the jewels taken from?
   a. Trinity College Dublin
   b. Dublin Castle
   c. Farmleigh House
   d. Newbridge House
4. True or false: Ronnie Biggs, one of the 15 robbers in the UK's Great Train Robbery in 1963, escaped from prison and had his face altered by plastic surgery.
5. What did Italian serial killer Leonarda Cianciulli do to the remains of her victims?
   a. She taxidermied them.
   b. She made savory pies out of them.
   c. She made them into soaps and teacakes.
   d. She burned their bodies and used the ashes for fertilizer.
6. What is the nickname for Jack the Ripper experts?
   a. Rippernatic
   b. Ripperuoso
   c. Jack of All Trades
   d. Ripperologist
7. The Somerton Man—the nickname for the mysterious dead body found on a South Australian beach in 1948—was believed to be:
   a. A Russian spy
   b. A jilted lover poisoned by his paramour
   c. A ballet dancer
   d. All of the above
8. A Glasgow, Scotland, serial killer got the nickname "______ John" after witnesses said they heard him quoting Scripture.
9. Elvira Manahan, a well-loved socialite who was murdered by her realtor in her home, was from which Southeast Asian country?
10. In Greece, what is illegal to wear when touring monuments such as the Parthenon and Acropolis?
    a. Brogues
    b. High heels
    c. Cowboy boots
    d. Flip-flop shoes

Sudoku #1

Fill in the remaining squares so that each of the numbers 1 through 9 appears exactly once in each row, column, and block.

1			5		7	3	8	2
2			1		3	6	9	5
5	9	3		2	6		1	
9		5		7				8
			4	3				
3	4	1			5	9	6	
6			9					
		9		5		1		
	1			6	4			

DID YOU KNOW? Rochester, New York's largest mass arrest happened in 1946. Instead of only arresting strikers at a public protest, the police arrested everyone in sight—200 arrests, including a dog.

Harvey's Casino Bomb Extortion Note

Decode this extortion note snippet that bombers sent Harvey's Casino and the bomb squad in 1980. For a refresher on how to solve a cryptogram, see page 9.

A	B	C	D	E	F	G	H	I	J	K	L	M
18				13							10	
N	**O**	**P**	**Q**	**R**	**S**	**T**	**U**	**V**	**W**	**X**	**Y**	**Z**
				1	9	7						

_5 _20   E13 _2 _24 L10 _14 _4 E13 _4   T7 _3 _5 S9

_15 _14 _12 _15   _23 _14 _21 T7 A18 _5 _21 S9

E13 _21 _14 _19 _6 _3   T7 _21 T7   T7 _14

S9 E13 _22 E13 R1 E13 L10 _16   _4 A18 _12 A18 _6 E13

_3 A18 R1 R1 A18 _3 S9   A18 _23 R1 _14 S9 S9

T7 _3 E13   S9 T7 R1 E13 E13 T7.   T7 _3 _5 S9

[S 9][_ 3][_ 14][_ 19][L 10][_ 4] [_ 6][_ 5][_ 22][E 13] [_ 16][_ 14][_ 19]

[S 9][_ 14][_ 12][E 13] [_ 5][_ 4][E 13][A 18] [_ 14][_ 20] [T 7][_ 3][E 13]

[A 18][_ 12][_ 14][_ 19][_ 21][T 7] [_ 14][_ 20] [T 7][_ 21][T 7]

[_ 23][_ 14][_ 21][T 7][A 18][_ 5][_ 21][E 13][_ 4] [_ 25][_ 5][T 7][_ 3][_ 5][_ 21]

[T 7][_ 3][_ 5][S 9] [_ 15][_ 14][_ 2]. [_ 5][T 7] [_ 5][S 9] [_ 20][_ 19][L 10][L 10]

[_ 14][_ 20] [T 7][_ 21][T 7]. [_ 5][T 7] [_ 5][S 9] [_ 14][_ 19][R 1]

[A 18][_ 4][_ 22][_ 5][_ 23][E 13] [T 7][_ 14] [_ 23][_ 14][R 1][_ 4][_ 14][_ 21]

[_ 14][_ 20][_ 20] [A 18] [_ 12][_ 5][_ 21][_ 5][_ 12][_ 19][_ 12] [_ 14][_ 20]

[T 7][_ 25][E 13][L 10][_ 22][E 13] [_ 3][_ 19][_ 21][_ 4][R 1][E 13][_ 4]

[_ 20][E 13][E 13][T 7] [R 1][A 18][_ 4][_ 5][_ 19][S 9] [A 18][_ 21][_ 4]

[R 1][E 13][_ 12][_ 14][_ 22][E 13] [A 18][L 10][L 10] [_ 24][E 13][_ 14][_ 24][L 10][E 13]

[_ 20][R 1][_ 14][_ 12] [T 7][_ 3][A 18][T 7] [A 18][R 1][E 13][A 18].

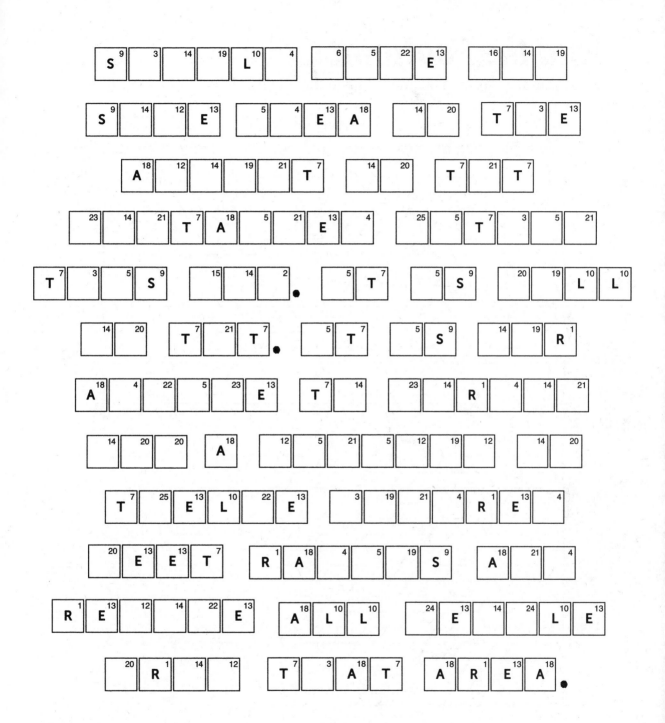

Find the Footprint

Make your way through the maze to find the muddy footprint of an escaped convict.

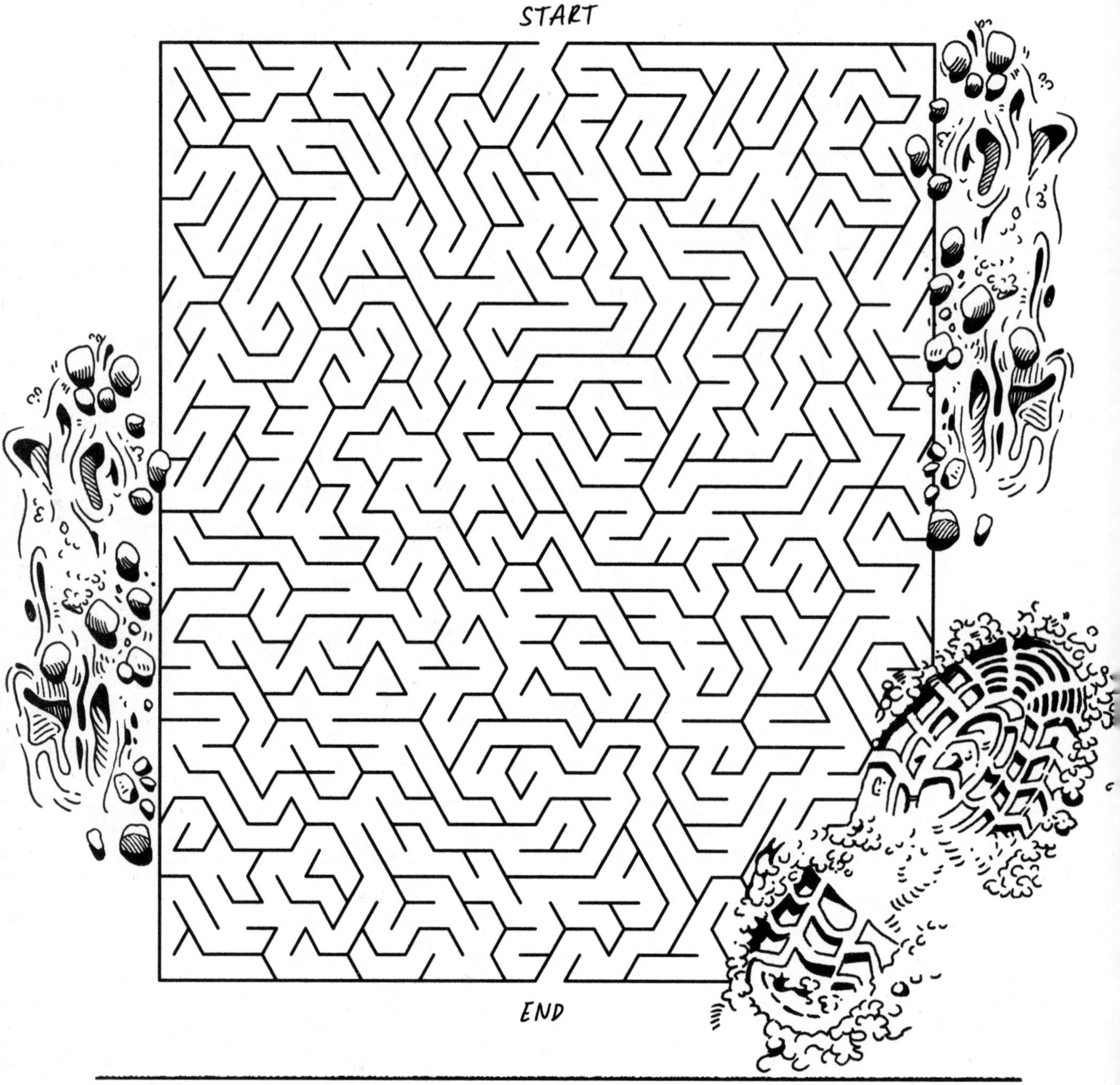

Magic Square

Using numbers 1 through 9, fill in the empty squares so that each row, column, and diagonal adds up to 15. Each number can be used only once.

#1

		8
9		1
	7	

#2

		6
3		7
		2

The Art of Stealing

Answer the questions to test your knowledge about famous art heists around the world.

1. The biggest unsolved art theft took place at the Isabella Stewart Gardner Museum in Boston after which holiday?
   a. Valentine's Day
   b. St. Patrick's Day
   c. Easter
   d. Halloween

2. The very first art theft was thought to have been carried out by pirates in what year?
   a. 1473
   b. 1612
   c. 1800
   d. 1902

3. True or false: In 1972, career criminal Florian Monday hid the paintings he stole in a hayloft on a pig farm in Rhode Island.

4. Which president's rare portrait was stolen from Polaroid Corp.'s warehouse safe in 1994?
   a. George H. W. Bush
   b. James Madison
   c. Thomas Jefferson
   d. Ronald Reagan

5. The world's first major oil painting, the *Ghent Altarpiece*, was stolen how many times?
   a. 5
   b. 7
   c. 10
   d. 13

6. On which social media app did the thieves of seven masterpieces from a Rotterdam museum meet?
   a. Tinder
   b. TikTok
   c. Facebook
   d. Instagram

7. True or false: A truck carrying 28 pieces of art worth about $6.5 million was stolen from a warehouse in Madrid because the keys were left in the glove compartment.

8. True or false: Los Angeles ophthalmologist Stephen Cooperman faked the heist of two art pieces from his home because he had recently lost his medical license after allegations of sexual harassment.

9. Which drug lord paid off disgraced NFL player Steve Kough with a Picasso ceramic art puzzle once owned by writer Ernest Hemingway?
   a. El Chapo
   b. Pablo Escobar
   c. Caro Quintero
   d. Griselda Blanco

10. What percentage of stolen artworks are returned to their original owners?
    a. 0 to 5 percent
    b. 5 to 10 percent
    c. 10 to 15 percent
    d. 15 to 20 percent

Sudoku #2

Fill in the remaining squares so that each of the numbers 1 through 9 appears exactly once in each row, column, and block.

	9		7	1		2	5	
	4		8			1		7
				9	6			4
1			4				6	9
3							1	
4	7	9		5		3	2	8
9	3			6		5	4	
	2	1						
	6	4	3		8			1

Black Dahlia

Unscramble the words that tell the story of the Black Dahlia.

1. slo neaglse

2. namilitout

3. labizhtee

4. odusvnel

5. unnqamine

6. drrmue

7. ydlowolho

8. wagolsg misle

The Great Maple Syrup Heist

Using the words listed in the word bank, fill in the grid.

Word Bank

barrel
barrel roller
Canada
fraud
heist
inside job
maple syrup
Québec
reserve
siphon
sticky
sugar
surplus
Vallières
warehouse

DID YOU KNOW? Québec produces more than 70 percent of the world's maple syrup. The heist from the warehouse was so large, it caused a global shortage of maple syrup.

Crime Scene

Someone's tampered with the crime scene! There are 10 differences. Can you find them?

BEFORE

AFTER

Futoshiki

Fill in the blank squares so that each of the numbers 1 through 4 appears exactly once in each row and column and the relationships between the squares meet the constraints of the inequality symbols.

#1

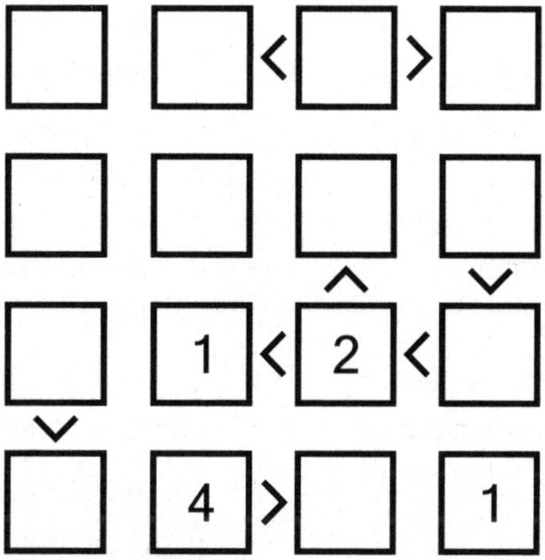

#2

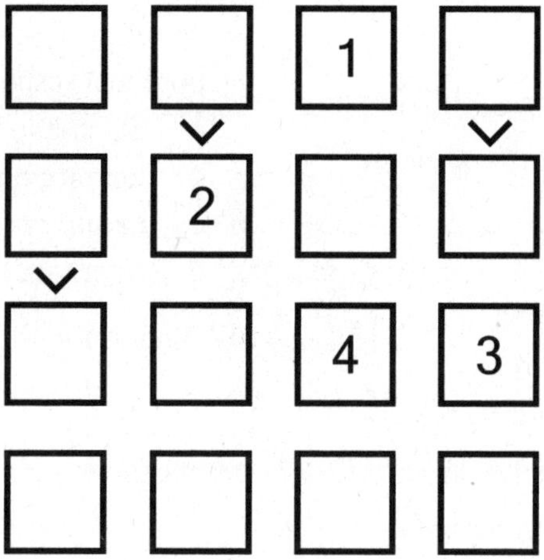

The CSI Effect

Answer the questions to test your knowledge about how to investigate a crime scene.

1. What are the four most common search patterns a police officer can use when doing a detailed search for evidence at a crime scene?
   a. Grid, spiral, zone, linear
   b. Crosshatch, linear, X-pattern, top-to-bottom
   c. Nonlinear, four corners, spiral, ray
   d. Quadrant, corner-to-corner, Z-pattern, grid

2. What application of scientific methods or expertise is used to investigate crimes or examine evidence that might be presented in a court of law?
   a. Criminology
   b. Forensic science
   c. Ballistics
   d. Pathology

3. A _______ is the person who says another person committed a crime against them.
   a. Suspect
   b. Defendant
   c. Complainant
   d. Witness

4. True or false: A chain of custody refers to the order that evidence is collected.

5. _______ are what an investigator uses to help them recall details from the crime scene when preparing an investigative report.

6. Deductive reasoning means to:
   a. Compare a case against past cases and create a hypothesis.
   b. Create a hypothesis about the crime, which is then tested using the facts of the case.
   c. Make multiple hypotheses and test them one at a time.
   d. Assume all cases can be explained by logic.

7. True or false: Reenacting the crime is NOT part of a crime scene investigation.

8. Locard's Exchange principle states that every contact leaves a _______.

9. Which type of prints are used to differentiate authorized people who may have inadvertently touched physical evidence from potential suspects?
   a. Elimination prints
   b. Latent prints
   c. Partial prints
   d. Alternate prints

10. What is the CSI effect?

A Collector's Dream

What do you call objects that are regarded as valuable because of their connection with murders or other notorious crimes? Solve the acrostic to find out!

1. The unlawful killing of a human being without malice
2. The entire cosmos
3. Criminal offense involving theft
4. Opposite of tidy or neat
5. Part of a crime scene that's essential for investigations
6. A musical composition for voices to honor the dead
7. Champion of a cause
8. Type of evidence found at a crime scene, often used for DNA analysis
9. Process of collecting evidence in a systematic manner
10. Main method of human communication
11. Point out, show
12. Cook's cover-up

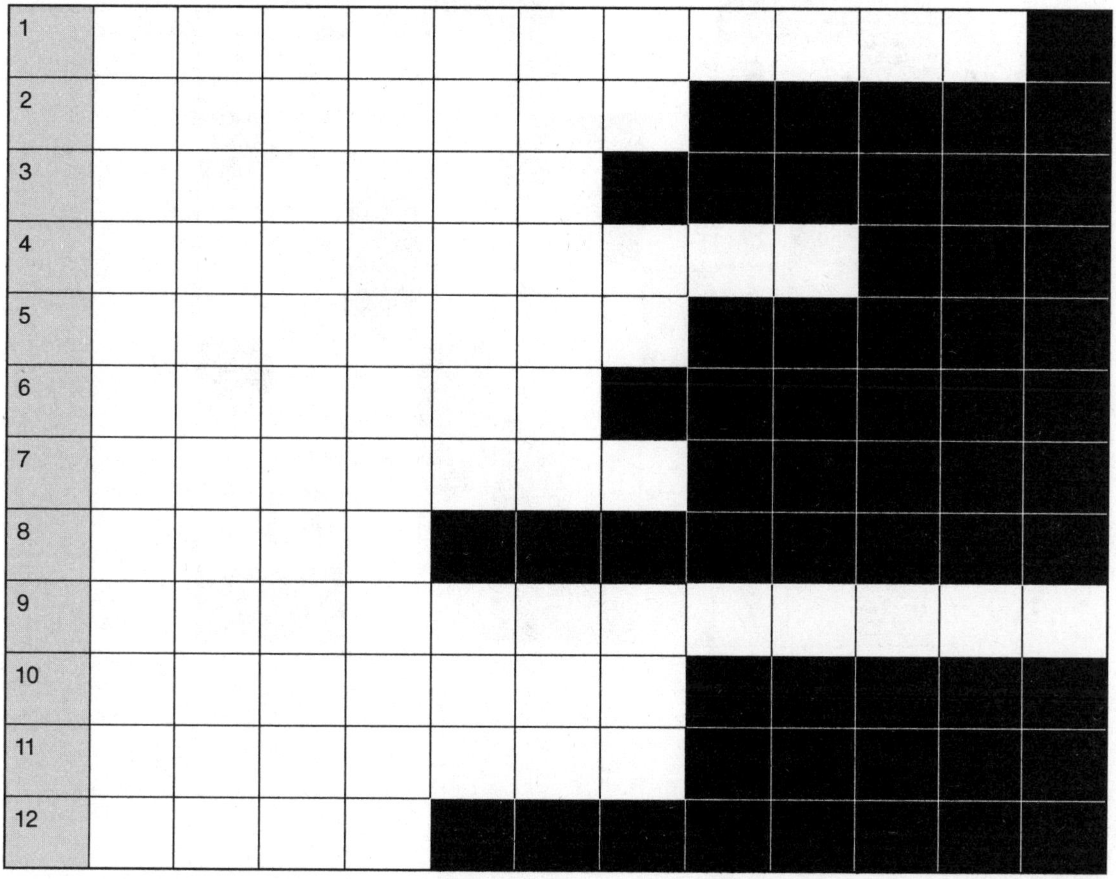

Kakuro #1

Fill in the blank squares with a number from 1 to 9 so that they add up to the given clues in the black, prefilled squares. Numbers cannot repeat in any across or down "run" of numbers. For a refresher on how to solve kakuro puzzles, see page 11.

An Escape Route

Follow the suspect through their escape route before they get away!

To Catch a Killer

Answer the questions to test your knowledge about serial killers.

1. Which of the following is NOT one of the three distinct types of serial killers as defined by the FBI?
   a. Medical killer
   b. Organized killer
   c. Disorganized killer
   d. Copycat killer
2. What does "BTK" in Dennis Rader's self-given nickname the BTK Killer stand for?
3. True or false: News anchor Tom Brokaw coined the term "serial killer."
4. What kind of evidence helped catch Seattle's Green River Killer in 2001?
   a. Cat hairs
   b. Clothing fibers
   c. Spray paint specks
   d. Fingerprints
5. Which of the following is NOT a known serial killer moniker?
   a. The Mad Butcher
   b. The Interstate Slayer
   c. The Killer Handyman
   d. The Co-Ed Killer
6. Peter Kürten was dubbed "The ______ of Düsseldorf" because he drank the blood of at least one of his victims.
7. Although Dr. Harold Shipman, also known as Dr. Death, was convicted of killing 15 people by injecting them with lethal doses of diamorphine, experts estimate that his actual kill count is between:
   a. 15–25
   b. 25–50
   c. 100–200
   d. 250–450
8. True or false: "The Hillside Strangler" let the daughter of Hungarian actor Peter Lorre go unharmed because killing a celebrity's daughter would bring unwanted attention.
9. Why was Lonnie David Franklin Jr. called the Grim Sleeper?
10. Serial murderers are frequently found to have an unusual or unnatural relationship with their:
    a. Mothers
    b. Fathers
    c. Sisters
    d. Teachers

Eyewitness Testimony

List all the words you can make from the letters in TESTIMONY.

DID YOU KNOW? Bank robber John Dillinger, deemed "Public Enemy #1," whittled a gun out of wood to break out of the "escape proof" Lake County Jail.

A Night at Raven Manor

Raven Manor Gallery had three art pieces stolen overnight. The police have five suspects, but they all have alibis that can be corroborated by a witness. Using the given information, can you match each suspect to their alibi and witness? For a refresher on how to complete a logic grid puzzle, see page 10.

CLUES

1. The art critic was not at home or organizing supplies during the time of the heist.
2. The security guard was not at a different gallery, which was proven by the surveillance cameras.
3. The gallery owner was either at a different gallery or seen by their neighbor.
4. The artist in residence signed in elsewhere during the heist, which was not in another part of the gallery.
5. The custodian claims to have been organizing supplies, but it was not witnessed by a neighbor.
6. The boyfriend was with the art critic at a restaurant during the heist.
7. The surveillance cameras in another part of the gallery picked up one of the suspects.

		ALIBI					WITNESS				
		at home	different gallery	at a restaurant	another part of gallery	organizing supplies	sign-in sheet	surveillance cameras	sister on FaceTime	neighbor	boyfriend
SUSPECT	art critic										
	security guard										
	gallery owner										
	artist in residence										
	custodian										
WITNESS	sign-in sheet										
	surveillance cameras										
	sister on FaceTime										
	neighbor										
	boyfriend										

Early Warning Signs of Serial Killers

Decode the cryptogram to learn the early warning signs of serial killers. For a refresher on how to solve a cryptogram, see page 9.

A	B	C	D	E	F	G	H	I	J	K	L	M
4	1			19								

N	O	P	Q	R	S	T	U	V	W	X	Y	Z
				3	6							

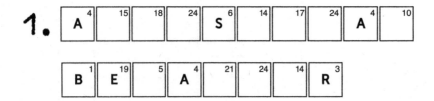

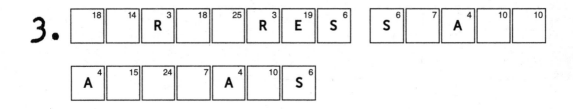

1.

4	15	18	24	6	14	17	24	4	10
A				S				A	

1	19	5	4	21	24	14	3
B	E		A				R

2.

4	3	6	14	15
A	R	S		

3.

18	14	3	18	25	3	19	6
		R			R	E	S

6	7	4	10	10
S		A		

4	15	24	7	4	10	6
A				A		S

4.

12	14	14	3
			R

9	4	7	24	10	11
	A				

10	24	9	19
			E

5.

17	5	24	10	2	5	14	14	2

4	1	25	6	19
A	B		S	E

6.

6	25	1	6	18	4	15	17	19
S		B	S		A			E

4	1	25	6	19
A	B		S	E

7.

21	14	11	19	25	3	24	6	7
			E		R		S	

8.

24	15	18	19	10	10	24	8	19	15	17	19
			E					E			E

9.

6	5	24	9	18	10	19	6	6	15	19	6	6
S						E	S	S		E	S	S

Sudoku #3

Fill in the remaining squares so that each of the numbers 1 through 9 appears exactly once in each row, column, and block.

3	5		7	1				
	9		6					7
		4						2
		3		5		4		8
		5			1	2		3
			2	4		7		5
9	4			6	7			1
	3	7	1	8		9		
5		1			9		7	

DID YOU KNOW? Social engineering is a manipulative tactic to convince people to divulge private or personal details so that the deceiver can gain access to a system or sensitive information.

Female Serial Killers

Answer the questions to test your knowledge about female serial killers.

1. How did police catch Aileen Wuornos, who shot seven men at point-blank range in Florida between 1989 and 1990?
    a. A victim's family member saw her leaving a victim's house and called the police.
    b. She was caught on a victim's security camera.
    c. She was captured after a minor traffic accident in one of her victims' cars.
    d. She turned herself in.
2. True or false: Juana Barraza was known as "The Old Lady Killer" because she was an older woman.
3. "Jolly Jane" was a ______ who killed dozens of patients.
4. Gesche Gottfried killed 15 people using ______.
    a. Arsenic
    b. Tainted alcohol
    c. A kitchen knife
    d. Rope
5. Which of the following was NOT one of Nannie Doss's monikers?
    a. Giggling Granny
    b. Lonely Hearts Killer
    c. Killer Grandma
    d. Lady Blue Beard
6. True or false: Dorothea Puente, the "Death House Landlady," killed her elderly tenants to collect their Social Security checks.
7. Before she became The Godmother of the murderous Narcosatanists cult that killed 15 people, Sara Aldrete claimed she first learned about the cults from ______.
    a. Online
    b. A newspaper article
    c. An anthropology course
    d. A TV show
8. True or false: Stacey Castor killed her husband with antifreeze.
9. Tillie Klimek claimed ______ accurately predicted the dates of her victims' deaths.
    a. Visions
    b. Precognitive dreams
    c. Spiritual messages
    d. Tarot readings
10. Linda Hazzard, licensed to practice medicine despite not having a medical degree, "treated" her patients via fasting, giving them only small amounts of ______.

Magic Square

Using the numbers 1 through 9, fill in the empty squares so that each row, column, and diagonal adds up to 15. Each number can be used only once.

#3

	9	
3		7
	1	

#4

6		2
8		4

Fingerprint Match

Find the matching fingerprint to determine which suspect was at the crime scene.

Case No.	7890-3165
ID No.	129
Description	Print pulled from murder weapon
Date filed	04-22-2024

Suspect 1

Suspect 2

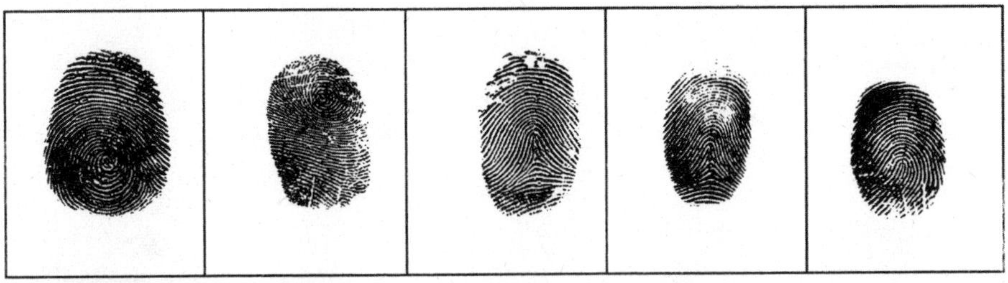

Suspect 3

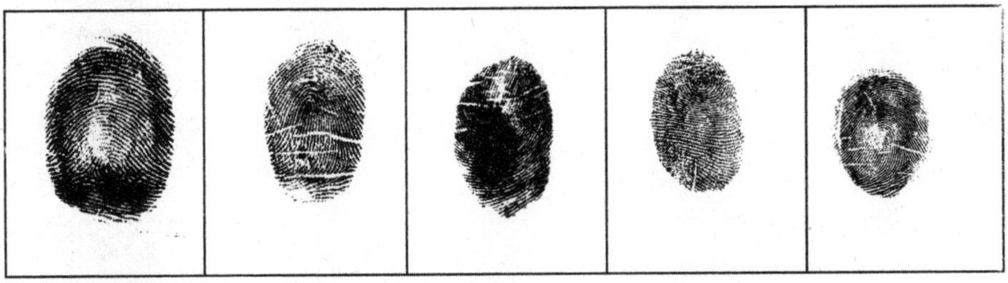

Suspect 4

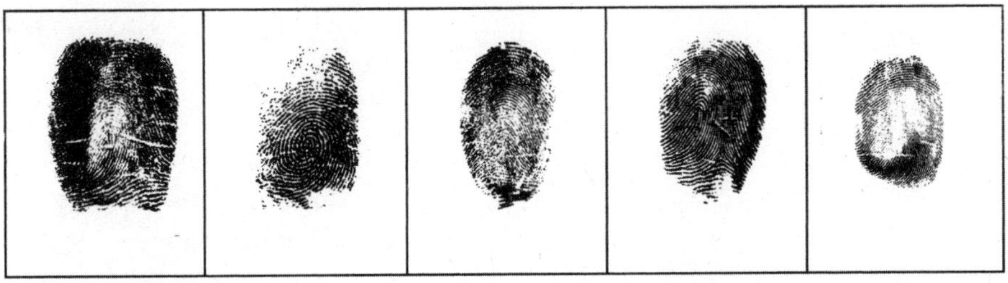

Loan Sharks, Gamblers, and Bootleggers—Oh My!

Answer the questions to test your knowledge about organized crime.

1. Which of the following are not one of the "Five Families" of the Italian American Mafia in New York City?
   a. Bonanno
   b. Colombo
   c. Gambino
   d. Luciano

2. The Mafia is also known as LCN, which stands for ______.

3. What's the name of the Mafia's sacred code of silence toward law enforcement?
   a. Omertà
   b. Il silenzio
   c. Segreto
   d. Sacro

4. In which Italian locale did the Mafia form?
   a. Rome
   b. Sicily
   c. Florence
   d. Naples

5. True or false: The leader of the Medellín Cartel, Pablo Escobar, was known for his lavish lifestyle, which included a personal zoo.

6. A Japanese organized crime group known as Yakuza has been in existence for more than:
   a. 25 years
   b. 50 years
   c. 100 years
   d. 300 years

7. Which of these was NOT a casino run by the Chicago Outfit?
   a. Stardust
   b. Desert Inn
   c. Luxor
   d. Riviera

8. The practice of using legitimate businesses as a cover for criminal activity is known as ______.

9. True or false: In 1973, the Italian criminal organization the 'Ndrangheta kidnapped John Paul Getty III, the grandson of an oil tycoon, and mailed his severed ear to a newspaper in Rome.

10. How do Japanese Yakuza members show their loyalty?
    a. Cover themselves in elaborate, complex tattoos
    b. Take a blood oath
    c. Spend a week in isolation
    d. Name their firstborn after a high-ranking member

Spot the Fake

Someone is trying to sell a forged piece of art! There are 10 differences between the real one and the fake one. Can you find them?

ORIGINAL

FORGERY

A Bad Investment

Across

3. Double your ______, or what the Greater Ministries International Church claimed their program could do
7. Sarah Howe, a fortune teller, convinced women to invest in her women's-only version of this institution
8. National pastime
10. Inexpensive
11. Rob ______ to pay Paul
14. None of the ______
15. A piece of art, often
20. Investor's goal
21. Occasion
22. Legitimate stockbroker who turned fraudulent (two words)
24. Lion sounds
26. Skimming off the ______
27. Abroad account

Down

1. The original scammer (two words)
2. Investor's consideration
4. Shortchange
5. Wall Street figure
6. *Wolf of* ______ (two words)
9. High-risk investment option (two words)
10. Make
12. More current
13. Give to charity
15. Rustic hotels
16. Too much of this may be too good to be true
17. US financial regulating agency, abbr.
18. DC Solar sold thousands of this never-made unit to big investors, promising federal tax credits
19. Bambi's mom
22. To defraud
23. Stocks and such
25. Church minister and radio host William Neil Gallagher, who bilked nearly 200 people out of $38 million, was also known as the ______ Doctor

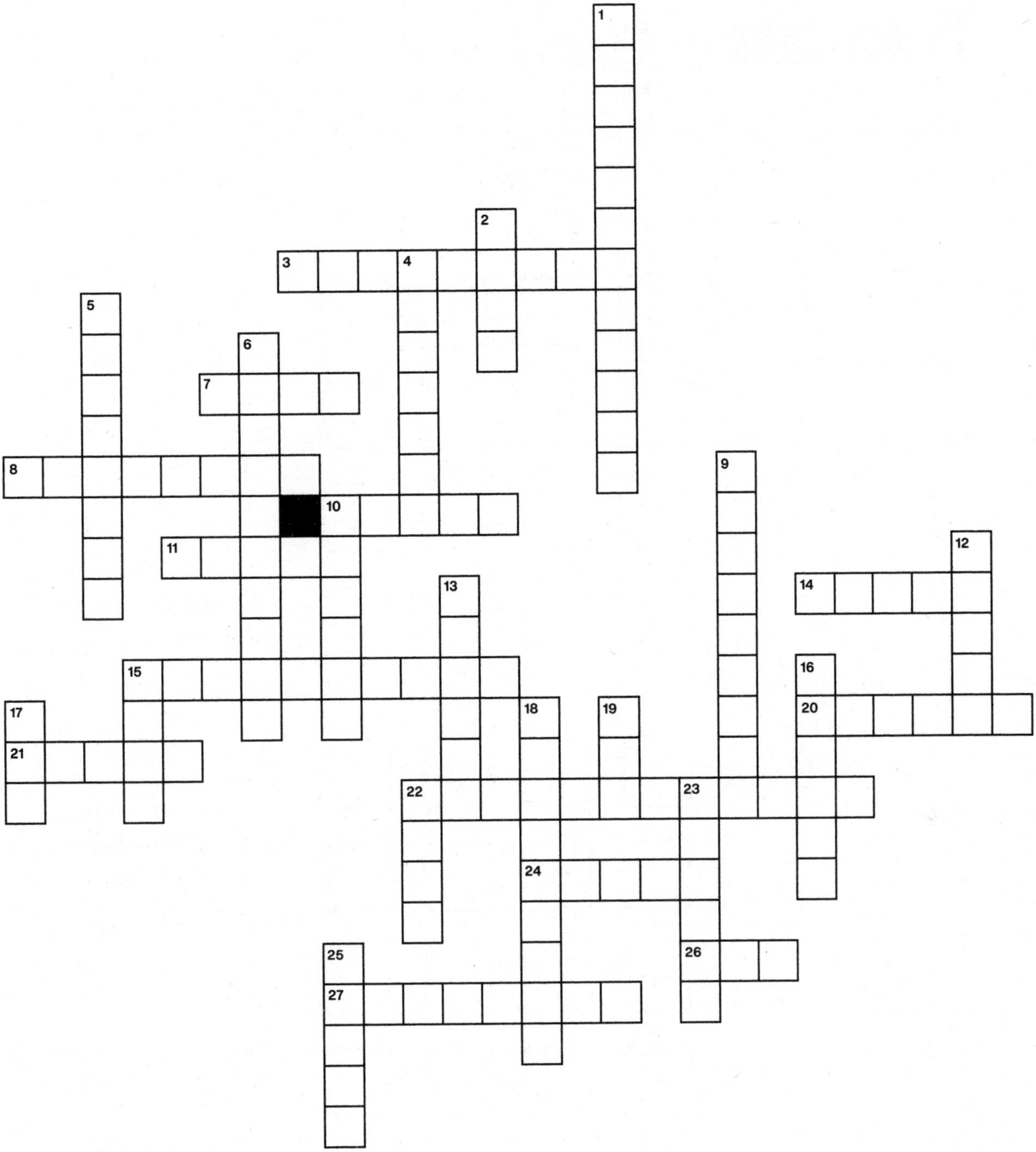

Futoshiki

Fill in the blank squares so that each of the numbers 1 through 4 appears exactly once in each row and column and the relationships between the squares meet the constraints of the inequality symbols.

#3

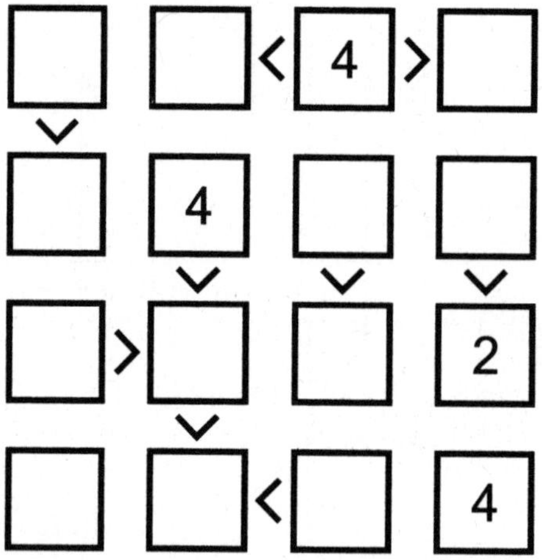

#4

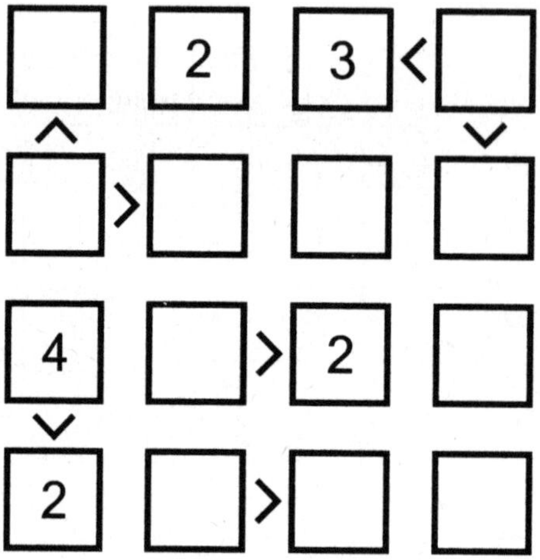

In the Valley of Ice and Death

What did they call the person found in Norway's remote wooded valley who had multiple aliases? Solve this acrostic to find the answer.

1. Manhattan, for example
2. Deliberate damage to hinder an activity or person
3. Advances in this technology have helped solve many cold cases
4. The White House, for the US president
5. This famous aviator's child was kidnapped and murdered
6. Online financial scam
7. Legal promise not to lie
8. Illegal work by a doctor
9. Aerial artist
10. "Not insignificant" is a double one

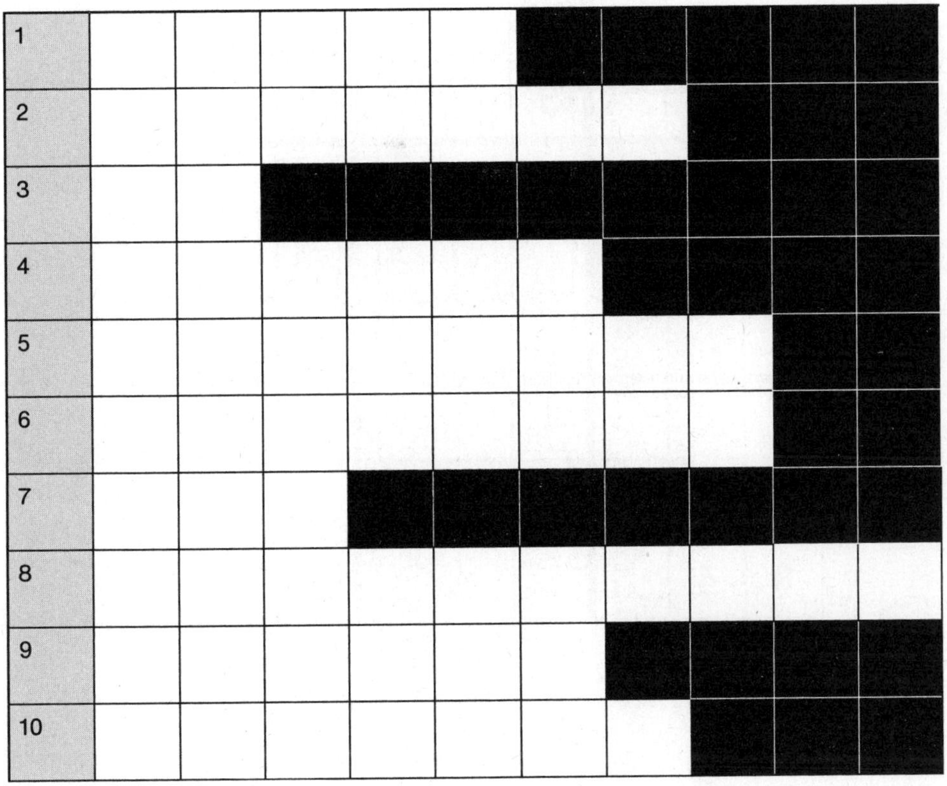

Sudoku #4

Fill in the remaining squares so that each of the numbers 1 through 9 appears exactly once in each row, column, and block.

4					8	3	5	7
3		6	2	1		8	4	9
9			5				6	
	8		3			1	9	
				7	5	6		
6						7		
	6		4		2			8
7	3		6				1	2
8	4							6

DID YOU KNOW? In September 1982, seven people in the Chicago area died from taking cyanide-laced Tylenol. These unsolved murders prompted tamperproof packaging for over-the-counter medications.

Land, Ho!

Answer the questions to test your knowledge about maritime crime.

1. According to the International Maritime Organization's 2022 Annual Report, where did the most instances of piracy and armed robbery against ships occur?
   a. Indian Sea
   b. Straits of Malacca and Singapore
   c. West Africa
   d. South China Sea

2. True or false: In the United States, most overt acts of piracy come with a mandatory minimum of life imprisonment.

3. Which of the following is a type of maritime crime?
   a. Tax evasion
   b. Human trafficking
   c. Unauthorized entry
   d. All of the above

4. The largest cocaine seizure in Spanish history was 9.5 tons of cocaine hidden in _______ crate containers shipped from Ecuador.

5. What is the name of the project Interpol has created to improve investigations into maritime-based crimes in the Eastern and Southern Africa and the Indian Ocean region?
   a. Project Compass
   b. Project Shipyard
   c. Project at Sea
   d. Project Helm

6. Illegal fishing includes all but which of the following activities?
   a. Fishing without a license
   b. Taking fish that are too small
   c. Using nets instead of poles
   d. Taking fish from another country's jurisdiction

7. International marine waters outside the jurisdiction of any country are called the _______ seas.

8. True or false: A country's territorial waters extend from the baseline to 5 nautical miles.

9. Which country has the largest maritime domain in the world?
   a. France
   b. United States
   c. China
   d. England

10. What nickname did Queen Elizabeth I give privateer Francis Drake?
   a. Sea Dog
   b. Francisco the Great
   c. Captain Fran
   d. My Pirate

Kakuro #2

Fill in the blank squares with a number from 1 to 9 so that they add up to the given clues in the black, prefilled squares. Numbers cannot repeat in any across or down "run" of numbers. For a refresher on how to solve kakuro puzzles, see page 11.

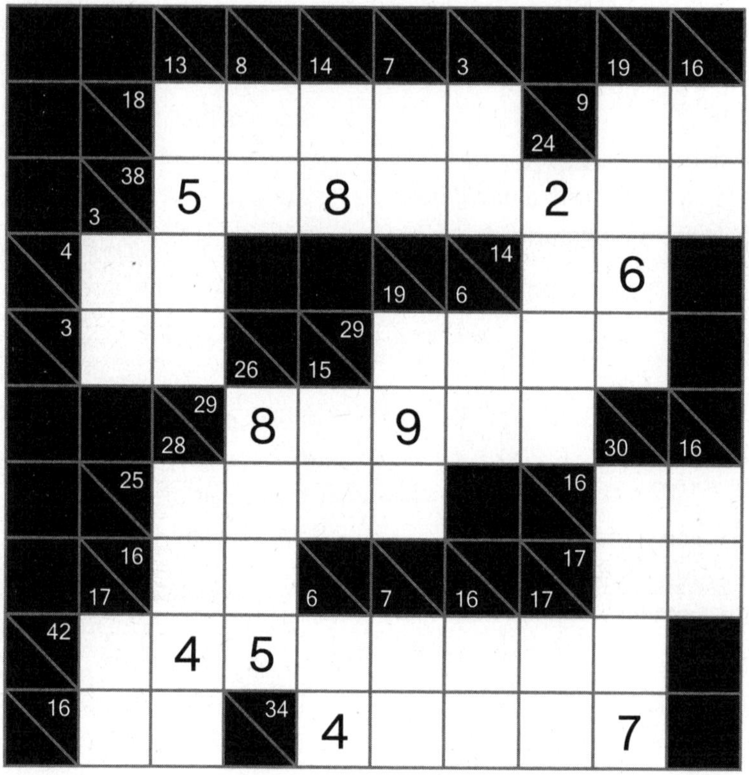

DID YOU KNOW? The FBI estimates that there are between 25 and 50 active serial killers in the United States at any given time.

Forensics

Find all the listed words in the grid of letters. Words can be found in any direction—horizontally, vertically, or diagonally. They can be either forward or backward.

I	G	P	H	T	T	Y	Q	Q	E	K	E	P	S	B	O	E	K	S	W	A	B	U
L	K	S	A	K	E	S	Z	J	Z	H	C	N	K	C	V	K	Z	N	E	N	C	G
N	P	L	Y	D	H	K	U	Q	E	R	O	Y	F	R	S	U	J	W	L	A	H	O
U	G	N	R	J	Y	B	C	D	I	I	R	J	I	I	S	U	T	H	T	L	A	R
D	Z	D	X	Q	Z	G	F	M	S	O	H	W	N	M	N	R	R	Q	M	Y	I	S
U	W	P	E	K	Y	K	I	S	T	F	Q	P	G	E	O	K	A	H	I	S	N	E
L	L	I	Q	T	Z	N	E	A	O	B	O	U	E	S	F	N	C	B	C	I	O	C
Z	B	T	T	W	A	R	R	R	L	A	F	D	R	C	C	E	E	V	R	S	F	N
I	I	C	S	L	P	O	E	O	E	S	U	N	P	E	T	H	B	M	O	U	C	E
P	R	Q	I	M	B	N	O	C	Z	Y	P	I	R	N	U	B	A	C	S	U	U	I
G	K	S	I	A	S	D	N	W	S	C	W	H	I	E	T	T	T	R	C	O	S	C
I	T	A	L	I	H	E	F	P	Z	F	H	Z	N	Q	A	L	H	D	O	K	T	S
O	T	K	C	D	D	O	O	F	B	Z	N	H	T	X	C	O	K	N	P	W	O	P
X	M	S	J	I	N	T	V	A	C	L	A	T	X	Q	X	V	O	F	E	V	D	D
S	V	B	V	K	U	A	F	A	T	S	C	I	T	S	I	L	L	A	B	B	Y	T
P	P	E	A	A	M	R	Y	G	O	L	O	C	I	X	O	T	W	Q	C	O	T	W

Word Bank

analysis
autopsy
ballistics
blood
chain of custody
crime scene
criminalist
DNA
dust
evidence
fingerprint
forensics
impressions
laboratory
microscope
sciences
toxicology
trace

Breakout

Answer the questions to test your knowledge about prisons.

1. What is the term used to describe a system where an inmate is temporarily released from prison but must adhere to specific conditions and report back at a designated time?
   a. Parole
   b. Solitary confinement
   c. Concurrent sentencing
   d. Trial

2. True or false: The United States has the world's largest prison population.

3. Alcatraz Federal Penitentiary was nicknamed ______.

4. In Brazil, inmates can reduce their sentence by 48 days per year by:
   a. Doing garbage duty
   b. Reading
   c. Cleaning bathrooms
   d. Gardening

5. Which amendment of the United States Constitution prohibits cruel and unusual punishment, including torture, within the prison system?
   a. Second Amendment
   b. Fifth Amendment
   c. Eighth Amendment
   d. Nineteenth Amendment

6. True or false: There are more colleges than jails in the United States.

7. What did Pascal Payet, who participated in the 1997 robbery of a Banque de France armored vehicle that resulted in the death of one of the guards, use to escape from prison?
   a. A hijacked helicopter
   b. A tunnel
   c. A laundry truck
   d. A window

8. Which of the following is NOT considered a major risk factor that predicts returning to crime (i.e., a criminogenic need)?
   a. Family dysfunction
   b. Low self-control
   c. Substance abuse
   d. Lack of employment options

9. ______ is the tendency of a convicted criminal to reoffend.

10. Prisoners at Northern Ireland's Magilligan Prison run this as part of a new environmental project:
    a. Recycling center
    b. Tree nursery
    c. Water treatment center
    d. Letter writing campaign

Forged Passport

The prime suspect in a case forged their passport. Can you find the 10 differences between the real one and the fake?

Texas Rangers

Unscramble the words that tell the history of the Texas Rangers.

1. satuni

2. roernitf

3. rpairie noltempar

4. dclasan

5. tcealt uetrrls

6. ilitmai

7. teotcnproi

8. lump recke

Notable Criminals

Answer the questions to test your knowledge about crimes involving celebrities.

1. Before he was an actor, Tim Allen was caught with this at a Michigan airport.
   a. A gun
   b. Counterfeit money
   c. Cocaine
   d. Fake ID

2. True or false: The UT Austin chapter of the Sigma Nu fraternity was disbanded on allegations of violent hazing by Jon Hamm and his brothers.

3. American boxing promoter Don King served time for manslaughter after killing his employee Sam Garrett. Why did he kill Garrett?
   a. Because he owed King $600.
   b. Because he stole something from King.
   c. Because he didn't show up for work.
   d. Because he thought Garrett was an intruder.

4. Operation ______ revealed a scheme to get the children of rich parents into top-tier schools with fake athletic credentials and bogus entrance exam scores.

5. True or false: On the eve of her release after serving time for tax evasion, singer Lauryn Hill dropped her single "Consumerism."

6. In what city was Kim Kardashian bound and threatened with a gun while a group of criminals stole jewelry from her?
   a. Los Angeles
   b. Paris
   c. New York City
   d. Milan

7. On what holiday was Harry Styles robbed at knifepoint near his home in London?

8. Which celebrity was NOT a victim of the Bling Ring burglaries?
   a. Lindsay Lohan
   b. Nicole Richie
   c. Paris Hilton
   d. Rachel Bilson

9. What item prompted a plan to kidnap, break in, and assault Frances Bean Cobain's ex-husband Isaiah Silva?
   a. A guitar
   b. A watch
   c. A car
   d. A vintage jacket

10. Actress ______ was convicted of grand theft after leaving Saks Fifth Avenue in Beverly Hills with thousands of dollars' worth of merchandise stuffed in her purse.

Sudoku #5

Fill in the remaining squares so that each of the numbers 1 through 9 appears exactly once in each row, column, and block.

	9	3	4	6		8		2
		8	9		3	1	6	
								3
6	8	7			4			
3	2				8	9		1
9	1				5		7	
	6	9						
5			8				1	
			5	2		7	8	6

DID YOU KNOW? Hair follicles contain a person's DNA, so careful examination of this evidence can help determine the age of an individual.

Evidence Board

Someone's tampered with the evidence board! There are 10 differences. Can you find them?

BEFORE

AFTER

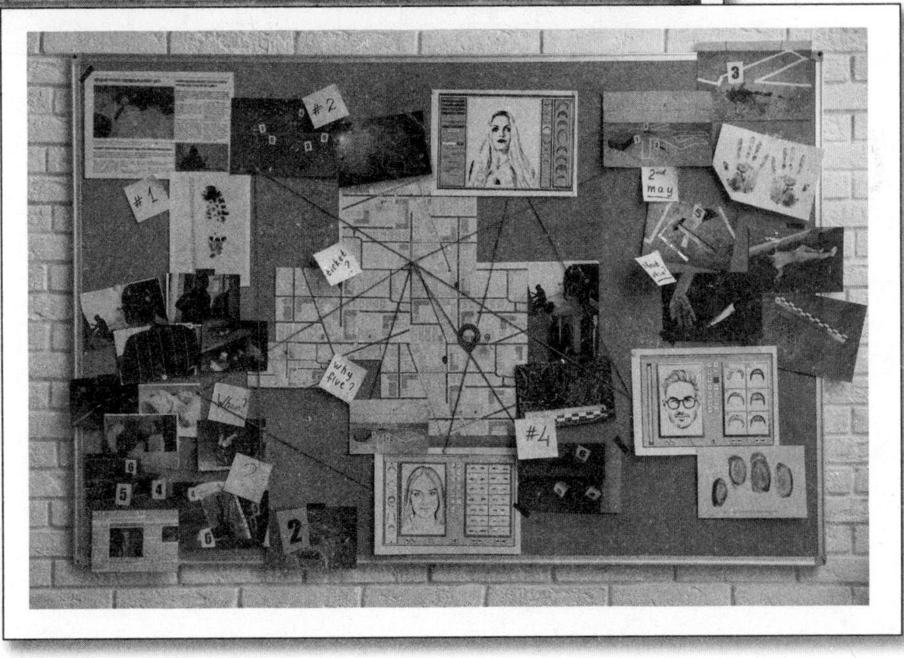

Letter from the Circleville, Ohio, Mystery Writer

Decode this mysterious, threatening letter sent to Mary Gillispie of Circleville, Ohio. For a refresher on how to solve a cryptogram, see page 9.

A	B	C	D	E	F	G	H	I	J	K	L	M
				26								
N	**O**	**P**	**Q**	**R**	**S**	**T**	**U**	**V**	**W**	**X**	**Y**	**Z**
20												

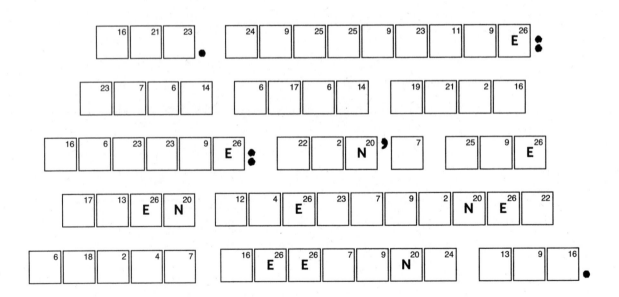

16 21 23 . 24 9 25 25 9 23 11 9 26 (E) :

23 7 6 14   6 17 6 14   19 21 2 16

16 6 23 23 9 26 (E) :   22 2 20 (N) ' 7   25 9 26 (E)

17 13 26 (E) 20 (N)   12 4 26 (E) 23 7 9 2 20 (N) 26 (E) 22

6 18 2 4 7   16 26 (E) 26 (E) 7 9 20 (N) 24   13 9 16 .

[9]   [3][N 20][2][17]   [17][13][E 26][21][E 26]   [14][2][4]

[25][9][5][E 26] :   [9] ' [5][E 26]   [18][E 26][E 26][N 20]

[2][18][23][E 26][21][5][9][N 20][24]   [14][2][4][21]

[13][2][4][23][E 26]   [6][N 20][22]   [3][N 20][2][17]

[14][2][4]   [13][6][5][E 26]   [10][13][9][25][22][21][E 26][N 20] .

[7][13][9][23]   [9][23]   [N 20][2]   [1][2][3][E 26] .

[11][25][E 26][6][23][E 26]   [7][6][3][E 26]   [9][7]

[23][E 26][21][9][2][4][23] .   [E 26][5][E 26][21][14][2][N 20][E 26]

[10][2][N 20][10][E 26][21][N 20][E 26][22]   [13][6][23]   [18][E 26][E 26][N 20]

[N 20][2][7][9][19][9][E 26][22] .   [9][7]   [17][9][25][25]

[18][E 26]   [2][5][E 26][21]   [23][2][2][N 20]

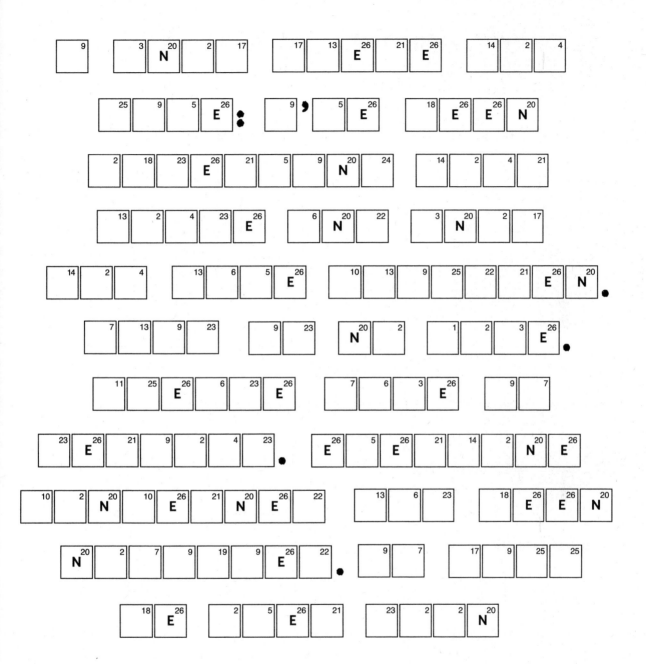

Criminal Justice

Using the words listed in the word bank, fill in the grid.

Word Bank

advocate
corrections
court
detective
due process
enforcement
investigation
judge
laws
lawyer
parole
patrol
police
sentencing
warden

DID YOU KNOW? The Texas Rangers may be best known for their bravery and protection, but they also forcibly removed Native Americans from their lands, refused people their right to a trial, and lynched Mexicans and Mexican Americans.

Magic Square

Using numbers 1 through 9, fill in the empty squares so that each row, column, and diagonal adds up to 15. Each number can be used only once.

#5

6		8
		3
	9	

#6

		4
1		9
6		

Bizarre Crimes

Answer the questions to test your knowledge about bizarre crimes.

1. True or false: In 2017, an unhoused Ohio man was arrested for breaking into a home. But instead of stealing anything, the man cooked food he brought with him and took a shower.

2. A Florida bride and her caterer laced wedding guests' dishes with ______ allegedly as a prank, but some guests had bad reactions to the food, such as vomiting and hallucinations.
   a. Marijuana
   b. Laxatives
   c. LSD
   d. Shrooms

3. An Australian woman stole a delivery van carrying 10,000 ______.
   a. Frogs
   b. Krispy Kreme doughnuts
   c. Mannequin heads
   d. Pencils

4. In 1986, the Bowen family noticed items moving and disappearing in their Massachusetts home. It was discovered that a ______ was living in their bathroom wall.
   a. Raccoon
   b. Squirrel
   c. Teenage boy
   d. Cat

5. Millionaire Marty Markowitz was manipulated by his ______, who persuaded Markowitz to give him power of attorney.

6. True or false: In 1771, a royal English maid named Sarah Wilson who was sent to America as an indentured servant after stealing royal jewelry escaped and convinced wealthy colonial families that she was Queen Charlotte's sister.

7. What is the reward for returning a stolen diamond-encrusted cheese slicer to Amsterdam's Cheese Museum?
   a. A platinum cheese slicer
   b. The world's largest commercially available fondue set
   c. Cheese for life
   d. A cheese board made out of the finest wood

8. What was the initial reason a woman became irate at a Florida pizza parlor in 2016?
   a. The pizzeria didn't sell Coke products.
   b. The pizzeria didn't have to-go containers.
   c. The pizzeria wouldn't let her watch the news on the restaurant's TV.
   d. The pizzeria incorrectly put cheese on her garlic knots.

9. What did a 36-year-old man do after he stole ammunition and sunglasses from a store?
   a. He returned the items.
   b. He applied for a job at the store.
   c. He called in his crime to the police.
   d. He came back to pay for the items.

H. H. Holmes's Murder Castle

Can you escape the Murder Castle without setting off any of Holmes's booby traps?

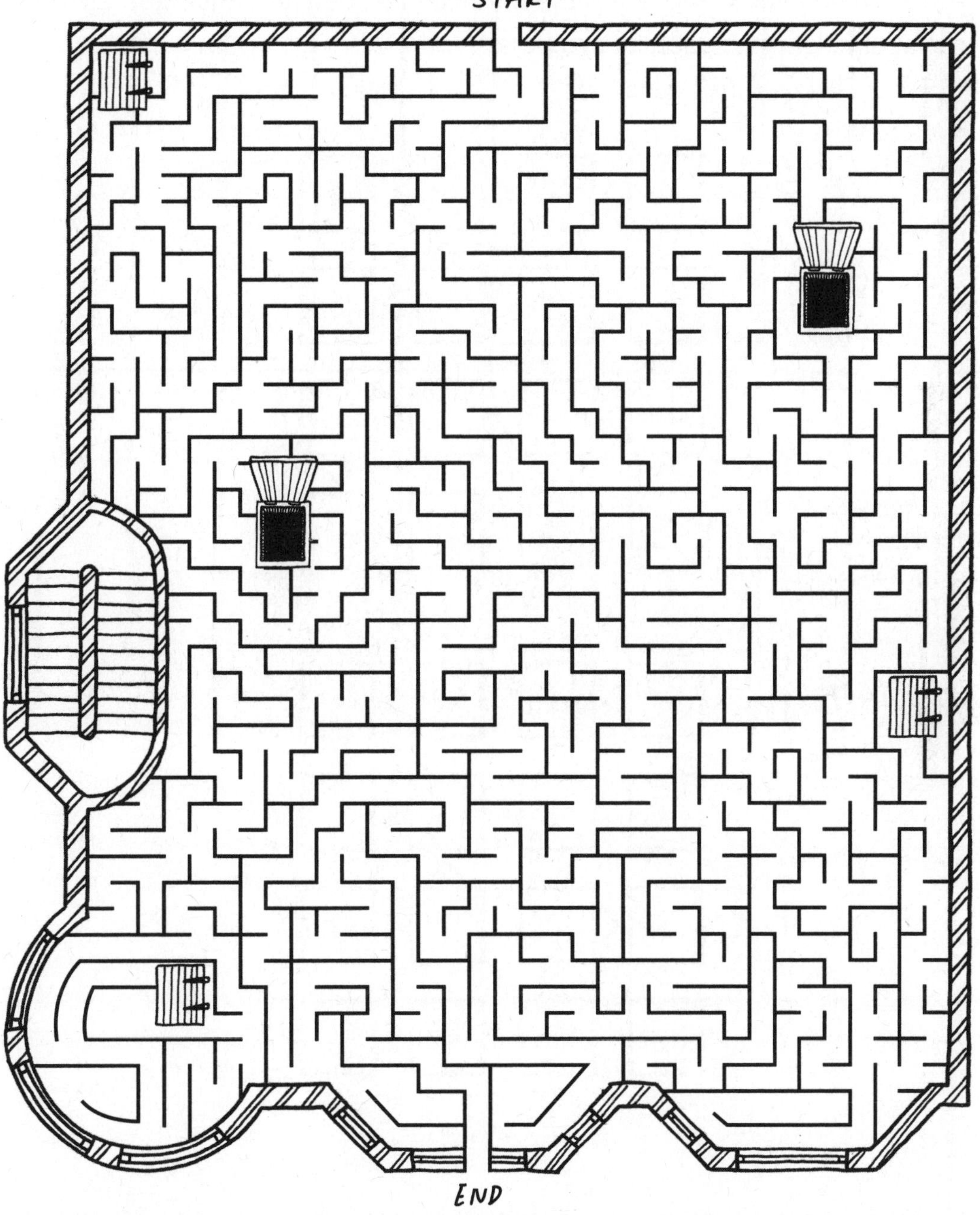

Futoshiki

Fill in the blank squares so that each of the numbers 1 through 4 appears exactly once in each row and column and the relationships between the squares meet the constraints of the inequality symbols.

#5

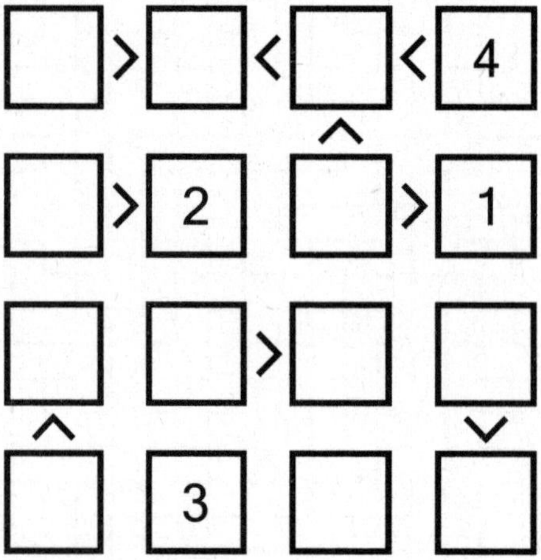

#6

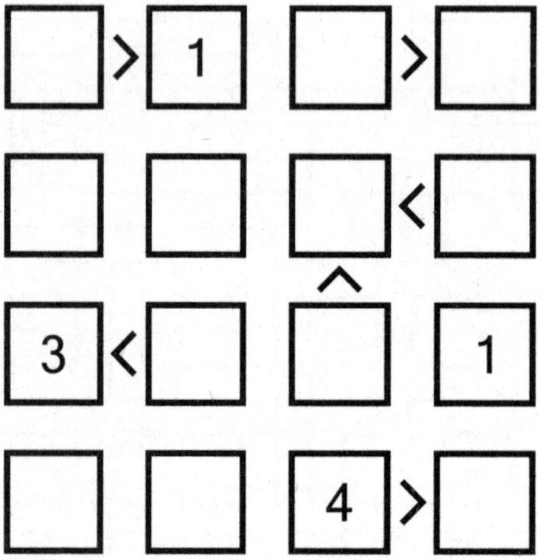

All Rise

Answer the questions to test your knowledge about what happens in a courtroom.

1. A writ of ______ is a court order demanding that a warden or other public officer produce an individual at court to show a valid reason the individual has been detained.
   a. Habeas corpus
   b. Ex parte
   c. Ad litem
   d. Per curiam
2. Who is the individual responsible for representing the government's case against the defendant in a criminal trial?
3. True or false: The judge chooses whether there will be a jury during a criminal case.
4. When does "voir dire" take place?
   a. During opening statements
   b. During jury selection
   c. During closing statements
   d. While the jury is deliberating
5. A ______ opinion is a written statement by a judge or justice who disagrees with the majority opinion reached by the court.
   a. Concurring
   b. Reviewing
   c. Dissenting
   d. Negative
6. True or false: An incorrect legal judgment is called an error of law.
7. Which of the following is NOT a type of state trial court?
   a. Superior
   b. County
   c. District
   d. Local
8. What legal term describes a formal charge or accusation that a person has committed a crime?
9. The two participants in a trial are called:
   a. Contests
   b. Sides
   c. Parties
   d. Members
10. A ______ is a formal request made by a party to the court for a desired ruling, order, or judgment.

Forensic Investigations 101

A student studying forensic science is researching different cases. Can you help them organize their notes by matching each analyst to their expertise and case? For a refresher on how to complete a logic grid puzzle, see page 10.

CLUES

1. The analyst working on the triple homicide case, who is not Ryan, is an expert in DNA analysis.
2. Paul, who is a ballistics expert, is not working on the drug bust or missing persons cases.
3. The toxicology expert is not Lana or Kristin, but they did work on the car accident.
4. The analyst using chromatography is working on a drug bust.
5. Manish is not an expert in toxicology or chromatography.
6. Lana is an expert in DNA analysis.

		AREA OF EXPERTISE					CASE				
		ballistics	chromatography	DNA analysis	impression analysis	toxicology	car accident	drive-by shooting	drug bust	missing persons	triple homicide
ANALYST	Lana										
	Paul										
	Ryan										
	Kristin										
	Manish										
CASE	car accident										
	drive-by shooting										
	drug bust										
	missing persons										
	triple homicide										

Exhibit A

List all the words you can make from the letters in EVIDENCE.

DID YOU KNOW? Lois Gibson, who holds the Guinness World Record for "The World's Most Successful Forensic Artist," has helped the Houston Police Department identify more than 751 criminals.

Sudoku #6

Fill in the remaining squares so that each of the numbers 1 through 9 appears exactly once in each row, column, and block.

	5			6			8	7
7			4			6		
6	3				7	4	2	1
8			2				4	
	6	7		4		2	3	
					3		6	
9				7		3	1	
	7	6	1	2	8		9	4
		4			5		7	

Tunneling for Reais

In what city did a group of people set up a phony landscaping business as a cover and spend three months digging a 256-foot tunnel to rob a bank vault? Solve the acrostic to find out.

1. Leave in a hurry
2. Abroad
3. Sid Vicious, "Son of Sam," and Tupac Shakur have all done time here
4. Labor union associated with Jimmy Hoffa
5. On every occasion
6. Legal action initiated in a court
7. Clear from blame or wrongdoing
8. Fervor
9. Taken into custody by law enforcement

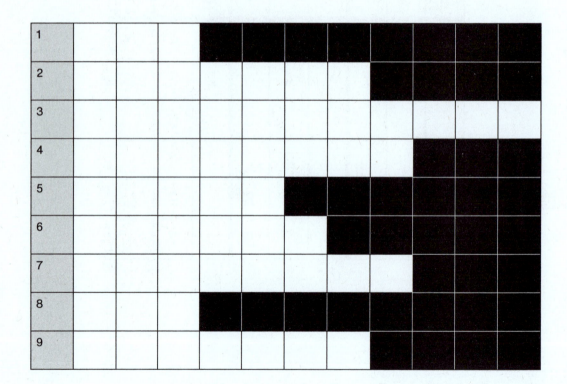

1				■	■	■	■	■	■	■	■
2								■	■	■	■
3											
4									■	■	■
5						■	■	■	■	■	■
6							■	■	■	■	■
7									■	■	■
8				■	■	■	■	■	■	■	■
9								■	■	■	■

Kakuro #3

Fill in the blank squares with a number from 1 to 9 so that they add up to the given clues in the black, prefilled squares. Numbers cannot repeat in any across or down "run" of numbers. For a refresher on how to solve kakuro puzzles, see page 11.

DID YOU KNOW? H. H. Holmes, one of America's first known serial killers, claimed to have killed more than 200 people in his Murder Castle. But experts now believe he may have killed as few as nine.

Unsolved Mysteries

Answer the questions to test your knowledge about unsolved mysteries.

1. What mysterious incident involved the sudden disappearance of a group of hikers in Russia in 1959?
   a. Bermuda Triangle mystery
   b. Roswell incident
   c. Dyatlov Pass incident
   d. Loch Ness disappearance

2. True or false: The Wow! signal, detected in 1977, is one of the most famous radio signals that has long thought to be extraterrestrial communication.

3. Several rumors circle around the disappearance of five of the Sodder family's children in a house fire in 1945. One was about how the fire chief tried to get the family to stop investigating. What did he do?
   a. Buried beef liver in the rubble and passed it off as a human heart
   b. Placed human bones in the ashes
   c. Bribed a coroner to say the children's remains were found among the ashes
   d. Claimed the children were seen leaving the house before the fire

4. What did a sketch artist include in the image of plane hijacker D. B. Cooper?

5. True or false: The mysterious "Axeman" of New Orleans used a specially made axe to attack his victims.

6. In 1935 at the Coogee Aquarium and Swimming Baths in Sydney, Australia, what item did a tiger shark vomit up that led police to a missing persons case?
   a. A bloody shirt
   b. A human arm
   c. A human foot
   d. A human finger

7. True or false: Hundreds of dogs have been lured by an unknown entity to jump off the Overtoun Bridge in Dumbarton, Scotland.

8. On March 13, 1997, a string of five lights in a V formation appeared in the sky above Phoenix, Arizona. Which one of these is NOT a way witnesses described what they saw?
   a. Orbs
   b. Triangles
   c. A singular massive craft that made no noise
   d. Lines

9. Michelle Von Emster's death in 1994 was ruled a ________ attack, but the sand found inside her stomach and the condition of where her leg was severed suggest otherwise.

10. The ________ was a vagabond whose identity remains unknown and who was famous for wearing handmade leather clothes and traveling between the Connecticut River and the Hudson River every year from 1857 to 1889.

DNA Sequence

Examine the DNA sequences to determine which sequence matches the one from the blood found at the scene of the crime.

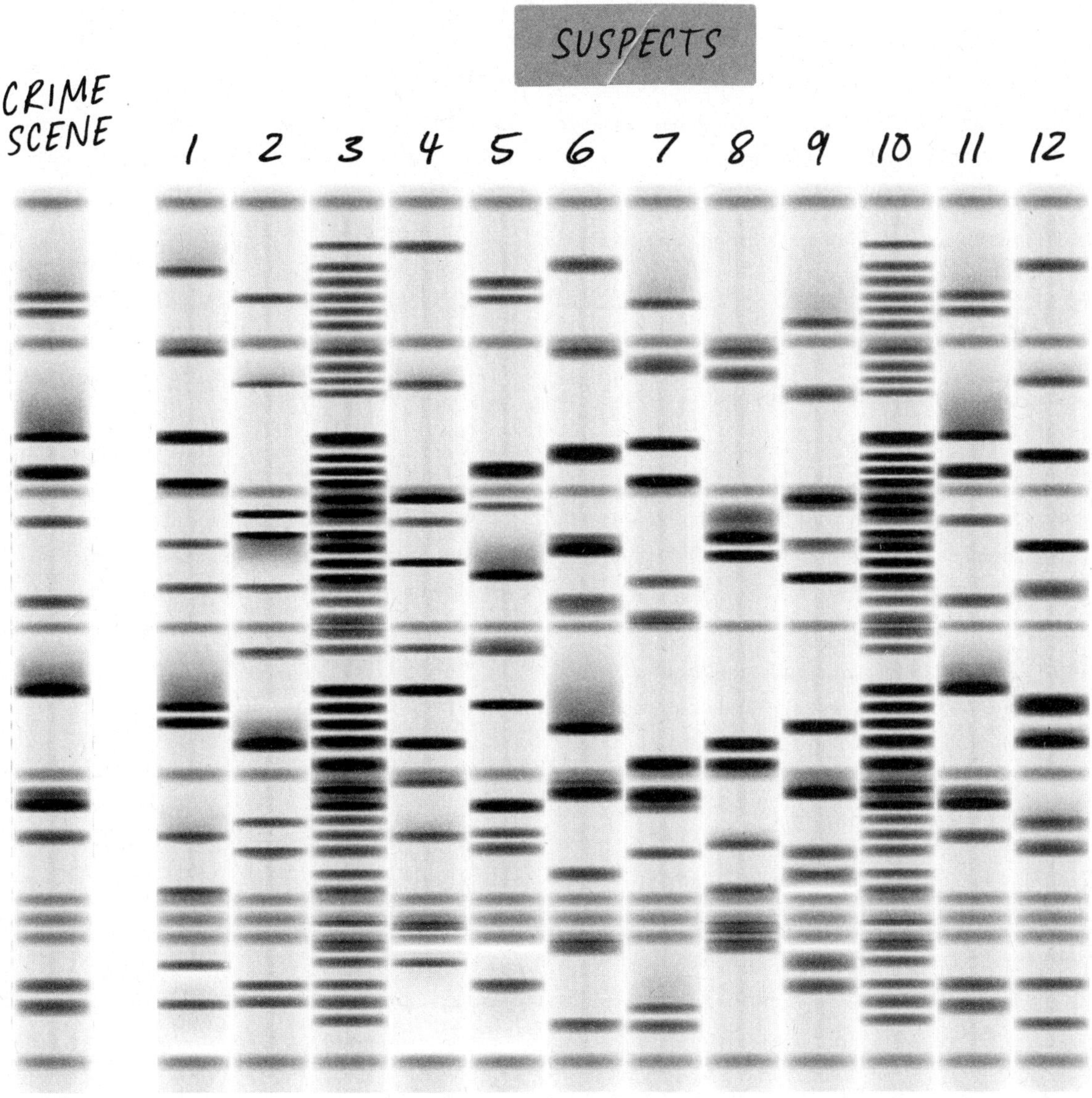

Cults

Across

4. Dance done in tutu and tights
5. Influence deviously
7. Acknowledged leader
8. The Branch Davidians prepared for this
10. Angel's Landing community members believe their leader to be one of these
14. Fenced-in group of buildings
17. Actor _______ Phoenix grew up in a Children of God commune
18. Fingerless gloves
20. Pisa has a leaning one
21. Heaven's Gate's salvation, abbr.
22. Take advantage of
24. 50 percent
26. Members of Aum Shinrikyo executed a chemical weapon attack in the '80s on a subway in this city
27. On the house
28. The Church of Synanon began as an alternative community in 1958 centered on group truth-telling sessions known as the _______
29. Vacation across the pond

Down

1. Satanic items, according to the True Russian Orthodox Church
2. Cult leader's asset
3. Fanatical
6. Adherent
9. The Family's leader, Anne Hamilton-Byrne, believed she was a reincarnation of _______ (two words)
11. Baby bear
12. Dominate
13. Building add-on
15. Sleepwear, informally
16. Belief
19. Cut off
23. Eggy holiday drink
25. The founder of the Japanese religious movement Honohana Sampogyo claimed to have the ability to diagnose physical illness by studying these
27. Violet, for one

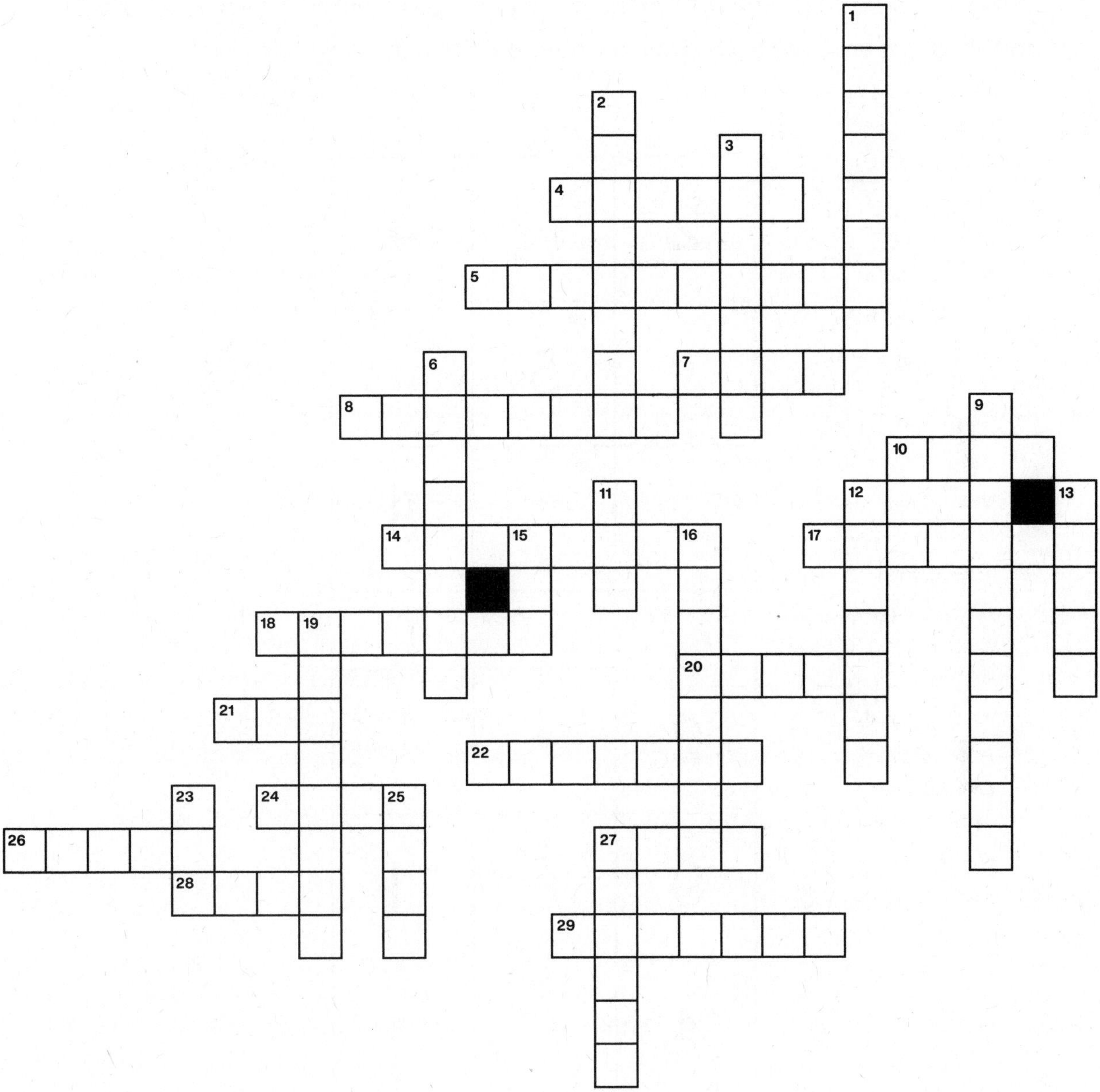
1
2
3
4
5
6
7
8
9
10
11
12
13
14
15
16
17
18
19
20
21
22
23
24
25
26
27
28
29

Magic Square

Using numbers 1 through 9, fill in the empty squares so that each row, column, and diagonal adds up to 15. Each number can be used only once.

#7

2		4
	5	
		8

#8

2		
9		1
4		

True Crime Media

Answer the questions to test your knowledge about true crime media.

1. Which of the following is NOT one of the ways a majority of surveyed Americans think true crime content impacts society?
   a. True crime makes people more empathetic.
   b. True crime helps people understand the criminal legal system better.
   c. True crime makes people more informed about the world.
   d. True crime makes people less empathetic.

2. True or false: "Missing White Woman Syndrome" is what late journalist Gwen Ifill described as mainstream media's fascination with portraying cases of white female victims while lacking attention for victims of color.

3. Which of the following is NOT the name of a TV series about true crime?
   a. *Wives with Knives*
   b. *Under the Porch*
   c. *Evil-in-Law*
   d. *Behind Mansion Walls*

4. True or false: 50 percent of Americans consume true crime at least once a week.

5. What is one of the longest-running TV programs and the first series to introduce a "call to action" that requested viewers to send in tips to help solve real cases?

6. Which case has been called England's "most literary murder"?
   a. The Radlett murder
   b. Red Barn murder
   c. The London Monster murders
   d. Jack the Ripper murders

7. Which dramatized true crime show became the second-most-watched English language series in the first month of its release, despite backlash from media consumers and victims' families?
   a. *The People v. O. J. Simpson: American Crime Story*
   b. *Dahmer—Monster: The Jeffrey Dahmer Story*
   c. *Love & Death*
   d. *The Assassination of Gianni Versace: American Crime Story*

8. What is the name of the victim whose murder is discussed in the podcast *Serial*?

9. Which serial killer prompted newspapers to print more salacious headlines and cover images to increase sales?
   a. Ted Bundy
   b. Boston Strangler
   c. Jack the Ripper
   d. The Yorkshire Witch

10. True or false: The Newport Beach, California, police department's podcast helped capture a millionaire fugitive accused of strangling his wife.

Types of Crime

Find all the listed words in the grid of letters. Words can be found in any direction—horizontally, vertically, or diagonally. They can be either forward or backward.

R	Z	V	I	M	S	S	M	R	H	L	G	T	D	O	N	N	K	N	T	H	C	T
B	C	L	X	L	F	O	X	Y	W	K	S	K	J	F	R	A	U	D	V	E	P	X
N	P	U	R	A	R	S	O	N	I	G	P	H	Y	O	K	B	W	T	E	H	T	Q
H	Y	O	N	V	V	A	N	D	A	L	I	S	M	Z	O	B	F	F	I	A	V	O
O	H	L	X	L	T	A	N	N	Q	Q	C	U	Q	J	N	E	T	S	X	U	L	W
M	P	A	C	Q	K	A	P	C	Q	G	X	H	O	U	H	R	H	E	M	N	V	V
I	Z	R	E	Q	P	T	O	B	J	T	A	P	R	T	A	I	V	F	V	M	Z	T
C	V	C	S	P	U	Q	R	W	C	C	U	D	Y	F	N	A	L	B	D	Q	L	F
I	M	E	I	E	I	I	P	Q	K	P	N	T	F	G	S	X	I	J	L	E	J	O
D	V	N	E	L	B	A	K	I	J	A	I	I	K	I	R	F	D	X	L	M	I	Y
E	G	Y	B	E	P	U	N	C	T	T	C	A	O	O	U	T	L	U	A	S	S	A
L	L	C	R	H	P	G	W	I	N	K	J	N	B	Q	T	S	C	A	M	S	H	L
O	U	Y	M	E	M	B	H	E	I	E	M	B	E	Z	Z	L	E	M	E	N	T	V
R	P	P	S	L	Y	G	D	N	V	X	E	N	V	V	F	V	Q	V	R	P	D	B
F	U	Y	Y	K	U	I	G	O	G	R	I	B	V	D	H	J	J	P	E	C	H	P
Y	C	N	A	U	R	T	E	W	Y	M	V	S	E	A	I	S	T	B	A	D	J	I

Word Bank

arson
assault
bribery
embezzlement
fraud
hacking
hit-and-run
homicide
identity theft
kidnapping
larceny
phishing
robbery
scams
tax evasion
trafficking
truancy
vandalism

Sudoku #7

Fill in the remaining squares so that each of the numbers 1 through 9 appears exactly once in each row, column, and block.

			8			1	7	6
5	6		7			4	3	8
		3		4		9		2
	8	6						
3	1			7				4
	5	4	9	2	8			
9	2	5		3				
6	4		5	8		2		
					7	5		

DID YOU KNOW? Detective Allan Pinkerton founded America's first detective agency, which had a logo of an unblinking eye and the words "We Never Sleep," from which came the term "private eye."

Blackmail Letter from the "Monster with 21 Faces"

Decode this letter from the "Monster with 21 Faces," who terrorized Japan with blackmail letters and tainted candies. For a refresher on solving cryptograms, see page 9.

A	B	C	D	E	F	G	H	I	J	K	L	M
				9								

N	O	P	Q	R	S	T	U	V	W	X	Y	Z
					20							

4 9(E) 5 1   20(S) 23 7 12 25 4   12 18 11 25 22 9(E)

18 19 19 25 22 9(E) 1 20(S) .   4 18 10 ' 23   11 25 9(E) .

5 11 11   22 1 25 24 9(E) 20(S)   16 9(E) 2 25 10

3 25 23 6   5   11 25 9(E)   5 20(S)   3 9(E)

20(S) 5 8   25 10   13 5 12 5 10 .   4 18 10 ' 23

8 18 7   21 10 18 3   23 6 5 23 ?   8 18 7

20(S) 9(E) 9(E) 24   23 18   16 9(E)   5 23   5   11 18 20(S) 20(S) .

Surveillance Camera Footage

Someone doctored the footage from the security camera. There are 10 differences. Can you find them?

BEFORE

AFTER

Under Attack

Answer the questions to test your knowledge about cybercrime.

1. Which is the most cyber secure country in the world?
   a. Denmark
   b. Sweden
   c. United States
   d. Japan

2. True or false: 80 percent of sponsored advertisements about puppies are scams.

3. Cybercrime is quickly becoming more profitable than the ______.
   a. Oil industry
   b. Diamond market
   c. Global entertainment industry
   d. Illegal drug trade

4. ______ is the primary point for 94 percent of malware attacks.

5. What new squad was formed at San Francisco's FBI after the "first online bank robbery" in 1994?
   a. Computer hacking squad
   b. Computer intrusion squad
   c. Online bank robbery squad
   d. Computer security squad

6. True or false: 25 percent of security breaches are caused by human error.

7. Released in 2010, the Coreflood botnet allowed cyber thieves to steal personal and financial information by recording unsuspecting users' every ______.
   a. Email
   b. Password
   c. Keystroke
   d. Financial transaction

8. How did the FBI catch graduate student Robert Tappan Morris, who unleashed the first major attack on the internet in 1988?
   a. Robert's friend spoke to a reporter and inadvertently referred to him by his initials.
   b. Robert embedded his name in the cyber worm he released.
   c. Robert turned himself in to the FBI when he realized how much damage his program had caused.
   d. Robert accidentally revealed his identity while bragging about his hacking skills on a national TV game show.

9. Which of the following is NOT one of the three main categories of cybercrime?
   a. Individual
   b. Property
   c. Corporate
   d. Government

10. ______ is the most popular form of cyberattack.

Kakuro #4

Fill in the blank squares with a number from 1 to 9 so that they add up to the given clues in the black, prefilled squares. Numbers cannot repeat in any across or down "run" of numbers. For a refresher on how to solve kakuro puzzles, see page 11.

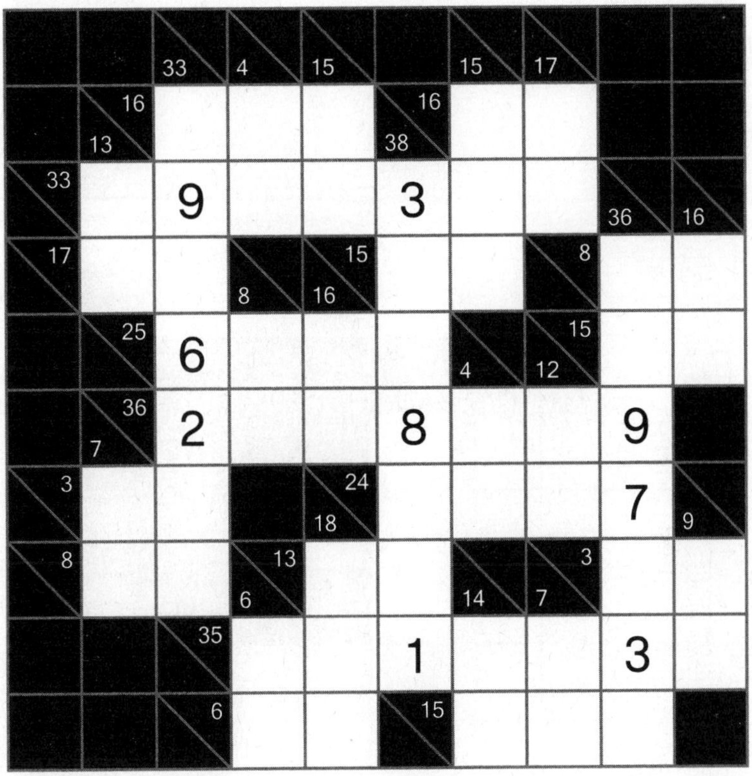

DID YOU KNOW? According to the Innocence Project, approximately 72 percent of 318 wrongful convictions were because an eyewitness misidentified someone. The real perps were later identified in 90, or 39 percent, of these cases.

A Priceless Treasure

What painting has had spray paint and a teacup thrown at it and been smeared with cake? Solve the acrostic to find out.

1. Member of a criminal gang
2. Bullfight call
3. Genre of film or literature characterized by its dark and pessimistic atmosphere
4. Childish Gambino, for example
5. Michigan, Erie, or Tahoe
6. Person who deceives others by assuming a false identity
7. Person under investigation for involvement in a crime
8. Writer

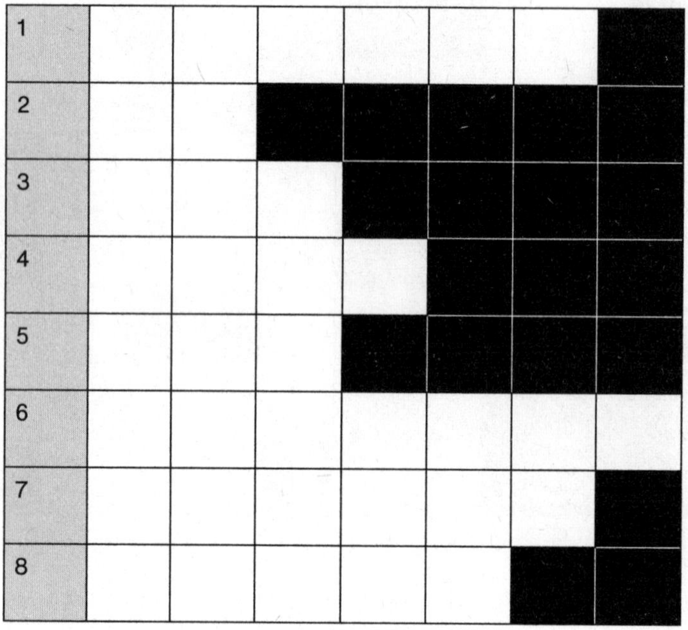

Coroner vs. Medical Examiner

Answer the questions to test your knowledge about coroners and medical examiners.

1. The word "coroner" in 11th-century England referred to an officer of the ______.
2. Where was the first-ever medical examiner office established?
   a. Suffolk County, Massachusetts
   b. New York City
   c. Philadelphia
   d. Baltimore
3. True or false: The first reported autopsy was of Julius Caesar.
4. True or false: Becoming a coroner requires formal medical training or forensic training.
5. What do medical examiners do?
   a. Review medical histories
   b. Conduct autopsies
   c. Relay findings to law enforcement
   d. All of the above
6. True or false: Medical examiners are elected officials who report to local government bodies.
7. A Tarrant County, Texas, coroner was suspended from doing autopsies in homicide cases after he mistook a bullet wound for a ______.
   a. Knife stab
   b. Surgical incision
   c. Puncture from a nail gun
   d. Self-inflicted injury
8. Coroners convene an ______ with a jury to investigate the death of a person.
9. Medical examiners originated in:
   a. England
   b. United States
   c. France and Scotland
   d. China
10. Milton Helpern, who performed thousands of autopsies and was internationally recognized as an expert in forensic medicine, was the chief medical examiner in 1954 in which city?
    a. New York City
    b. Boston
    c. Dallas
    d. Los Angeles

Sticky Fingers

Navigate your way through this unique maze.

Sudoku #8

Fill in the remaining squares so that each of the numbers 1 through 9 appears exactly once in each row, column, and block.

2				4				
7	4			5		2	8	1
			8	7			4	3
3	6			8	4	9		5
		1		6	5		7	4
				1	3	8		
	5		4	9	8			
	7	4			6			8
		3				4	5	

DID YOU KNOW? The first mass fingerprinting operation happened in 1948 when British police ordered all men over the age of 16 in the Lancashire town of Blackburn to submit their fingerprints to try to catch a child's murderer.

The Great Train Robbery

Using the words listed in the word bank, fill in the grid.

Word Bank

bank notes
Bridego Bridge
Bruce Reynolds
cash
England
fifteen
fingerprints
heist
holdup
Land Rovers
Leatherslade
loot
mail

Cecil Hotel

Unscramble the words that tell the history of the Cecil Hotel.

1. macbaer

2. rdumer

3. skdi rwo

4. thgin lterska

5. ivelenco

6. cbkla aalhid

7. aizrbre

8. enoipg ydla

Futoshiki

Fill in the blank squares so that each of the numbers 1 through 4 appears exactly once in each row and column and the relationships between the squares meet the constraints of the inequality symbols.

#7

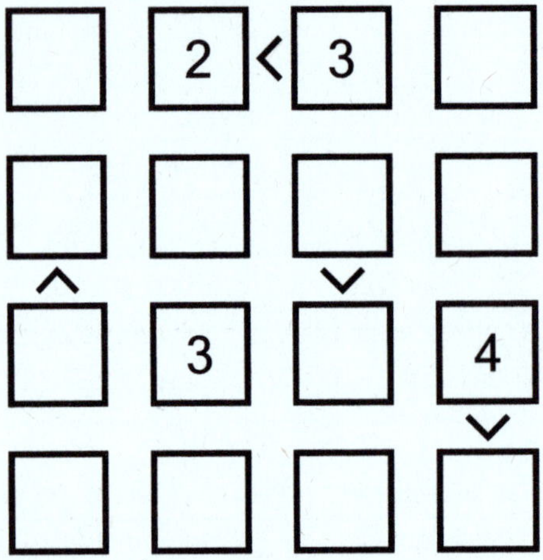

#8

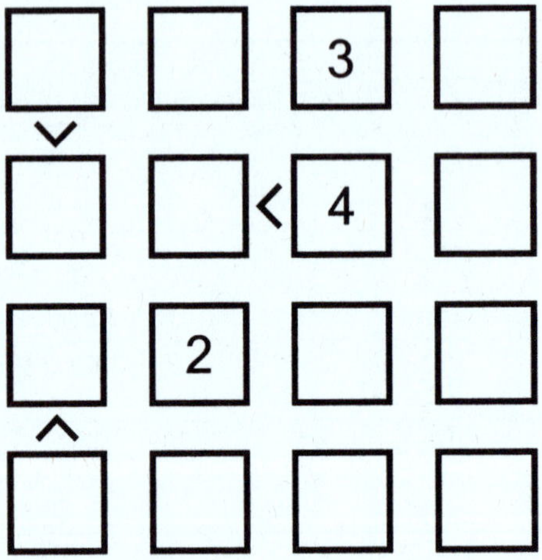

True Crime and Pop Culture

Answer the questions to test your knowledge about the intersection of true crime and pop culture.

1. Serial killer Ed Gein was not the inspiration for which fictional character?
    a. *Psycho*'s Norman Bates
    b. *Silence of the Lamb*'s Buffalo Bill
    c. *Texas Chainsaw Massacre*'s Leatherface
    d. *Child's Play*'s Charles Lee Ray
2. True or false: "The Kansas City Butcher" Bob Berdella claimed that the movie adaptation of John Fowles's 1963 novel *The Collector* had a huge impact on him as a teenager and served as inspiration for his crimes.
3. What 1949 television show romanticized the Texas Rangers and overshadowed their previous misdeeds?
4. Which video game was at the center of an alleged real-world roleplaying cult whose members believed they were reincarnated characters from the game?
    a. *Final Fantasy VII*
    b. *The Elder Scrolls V: Skyrim*
    c. *Diablo II*
    d. *Fallout*
5. Which serial killer did pop star Kesha include in a verse in her song "Cannibal"?
    a. Ed Gein
    b. Albert Fish
    c. Jeffrey Dahmer
    d. Ottis Toole
6. Charles Manson's misinterpretation of lyrics from which Beatles album served as his motive for killing Sharon Tate and Leno and Rosemary LaBianca?
    a. *Yellow Submarine*
    b. *White Album*
    c. *Abbey Road*
    d. *Sgt. Pepper's Lonely Hearts Club Band*
7. True or false: The TV show *Stranger Things* was inspired by Project MKUltra, a mind control program launched by the CIA in 1953.
8. Which of the following is NOT a slogan of the podcast *My Favorite Murder*?
    a. "You're in a cult; call your dad."
    b. "Stay out of the forest."
    c. "Don't go upstairs."
    d. "Stay sexy and don't get murdered."
9. Which novel has been closely associated with John Lennon's killer Mark David Chapman, would-be Ronald Reagan assassin John Hinckley Jr., and actress and model Rebecca Schaeffer's murderer Robert John Bardo?
10. True or false: The song "Midnight Rambler" by the Rolling Stones is about the Night Stalker.

Seized Jewelry

During the execution of a search warrant, police recovered several valuable stolen items. Can you find the 10 differences between these two images?

DID YOU KNOW? Civil asset forfeiture is the policy that allows police to seize any property they allege is involved in a crime even if the person has not been arrested or convicted of a crime.

Magic Square

Using the numbers 1 through 16, fill in the empty squares so that each row, column, and diagonal adds up to 34. Each number can be used only once.

#9

	15	14	
	10	7	
	8	9	
16			

#10

3			12
			2
8	1		
14	4		

'70s Crime

Answer the questions to test your knowledge about crimes that took place in the 1970s.

1. What did Manson Family member Lynette "Squeaky" Fromme do in an attempt to live out Charles Manson's "Helter Skelter" message even after he was convicted of murder?
2. True or false: "The Hillside Strangler," who killed ten young women and scattered their bodies among the hills of Los Angeles, was never captured.
3. What event led to media heiress Patty Hearst becoming an accomplice to crimes and spending two years in jail?
4. What object was suspected to have been used to bludgeon *Hogan's Heroes* actor Bob Crane despite no physical evidence?
5. True or false: The San Francisco killer "The Doodler" was given this moniker because he would draw temporary tattoos on his victims.
6. Which is NOT a theory about what happened to labor union president Jimmy Hoffa?
   a. He's buried under Section 107 of Giants Stadium.
   b. He was ground up in little pieces and thrown into a Florida swamp.
   c. He's in the witness protection program.
   d. He's buried in a steel drum in a New Jersey landfill.
7. What is significant about the Frederick Valentich Incident in Australia?
   a. It's theorized that the young pilot Frederick Valentich was captured by a UFO.
   b. It was an exhibition that featured all stolen art.
   c. It was a culinary event that purposefully gave guests food poisoning.
   d. It was the biggest illegal gambling event in cricket history.
8. Between October and November 1977, a series of seemingly random ______ would kill and injure multiple people, including Shirley Marie Flynn and Robert Curtis Jackson, in South County, Missouri.
9. What piece of forensic evidence in 2014 finally brought justice for the family of twelve-year-old Sheila and ten-year-old Katherine Lyon, who disappeared from a Maryland shopping mall in 1975?
   a. A letter stating the details of the crime
   b. Copious amounts of blood on the walls of the basement of the killer's father's home
   c. Bloody clothes stashed in the attic of the killer's aunt's house
   d. Fingerprints on a weapon found near the victims' remains

Gentleman of the Road

List all the words you can make from the letters in HIGHWAYMAN.

DID YOU KNOW? Highwaymen have often been romanticized in popular culture, and some even became folk heroes despite their criminal activities, like the fictional Robin Hood and real-life highwayman Claude Duval.

Heist Mix-Up

Detective Deedlebaum is doing some research on real heists, but all her information is mixed up. Use the clues provided to figure out where each heist occurred, the year it happened, and what was stolen. For a refresher on how to solve a logic grid puzzle, see page 10.

CLUES

1. The heist that took place in 1983 wasn't the one where works of art were stolen or the one that took place in Sweden.
2. The heist in Belgium wasn't in 1994 or 2018, but it did involve the theft of diamonds.
3. The Strängnäs Cathedral heist wasn't the heist where cash was stolen or the one in London, but it was in either 1994 or 2018.
4. The theft in Fortaleza didn't involve royal jewels or artwork but did happen at the Banco Central.
5. The Brink's-Mat Warehouse heist occurred in 1983 in London.
6. The Antwerp Vault heist was the heist where the robbers stole diamonds, but not in Sweden.
7. The heist in Fortaleza wasn't the one where gold bars were stolen.
8. The Isabella Stewart Gardner Museum heist wasn't in 2018 or in Sweden.
9. The gold bars were stolen in 1983 and the cash in 2005.
10. The works of art were stolen from the Isabella Stewart Gardner Museum.

HEIST	LOCATION					STOLEN ITEM					YEAR				
	Boston	Sweden	London	Belgium	Fortaleza	gold bars	works of art	royal jewels	diamonds	cash	1983	1994	2003	2005	2018
Brink's-Mat Warehouse															
Antwerp Vault															
Isabella Stewart Gardner Museum															
Banco Central burglary															
The Strängnäs Cathedral															

YEAR	Boston	Sweden	London	Belgium	Fortaleza	gold bars	works of art	royal jewels	diamonds	cash
1983										
1994										
2003										
2005										
2018										

STOLEN ITEM	Boston	Sweden	London	Belgium	Fortaleza
gold bars					
works of art					
royal jewels					
diamonds					
cash					

D. B. Cooper Hijacking Note

Decode the cryptogram to figure out D. B. Cooper's demands. For a refresher on solving cryptograms, see page 9.

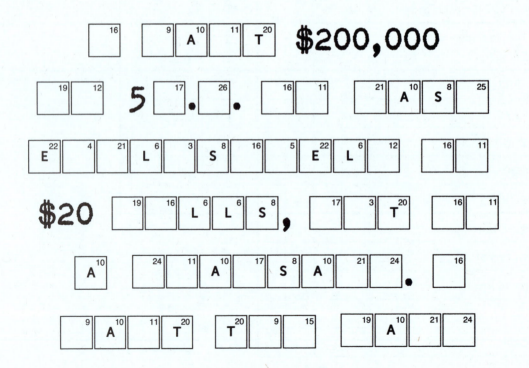

A	B	C	D	E	F	G	H	I	J	K	L	M
10				22							6	
N	**O**	**P**	**Q**	**R**	**S**	**T**	**U**	**V**	**W**	**X**	**Y**	**Z**
				13	8	20						

[16]   [9][A 10][11][T 20] $200,000

[19][12]   5[17].[26].   [16][11]   [21][A 10][S 8][25]

[E 22][4][21][L 6][3][S 8][16][5][E 22][L 6][12]   [16][11]

$20   [19][16][L 6][L 6][S 8],   [17][3][T 20]   [16][11]

[A 10]   [24][11][A 10][17][S 8][A 10][21][24].   [16]

[9][A 10][11][T 20]   [T 20][9][15]   [19][A 10][21][24]

[17][A 10][R 13][A 10][21][25][3][T 20][E 22][S 8] [A 10][11][1]

[T 20][9][15] [14][R 13][15][11][T 20]

[17][A 10][R 13][A 10][21][25][3][T 20][E 22][S 8]. [9][25][E 22][11]

[9][E 22] [L 6][A 10][11][1], [16] [9][A 10][11][T 20]

[A 10] [14][3][E 22][L 6] [T 20][R 13][3][21][24]

[R 13][E 22][A 10][1][12] [T 20][15] [R 13][E 22][14][3][E 22][L 6].

[11][15] [14][3][11][11][12] [S 8][T 20][3][14][14] [15][R 13]

[16]'[L 6][L 6] [1][15] [T 20][25][E 22] [2][15][19].

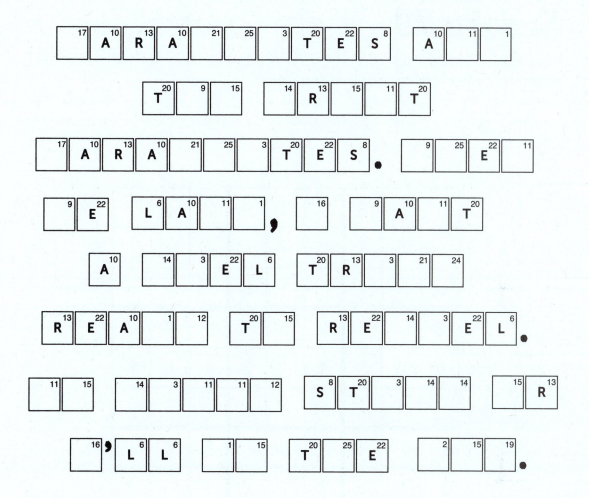

Sudoku #9

Fill in the remaining squares so that each of the numbers 1 through 9 appears exactly once in each row, column, and block.

		9		3	4	2		
	8							
		7		1	8			
8		4	9	5			2	7
7	6		1		3	4	8	
		2		4			5	
		1		9		8	6	
	5	8	4			7		2
		6		8		3	1	5

Do You Swear to Tell the Truth?

Review the polygraph results and find the one that matches.

POLYGRAPH RESULTS

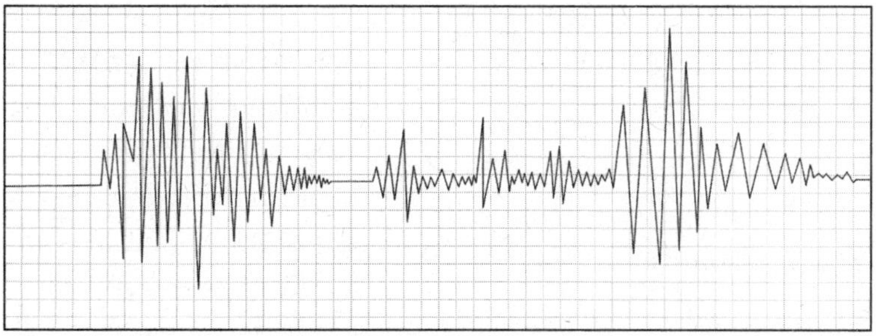

1

2

3

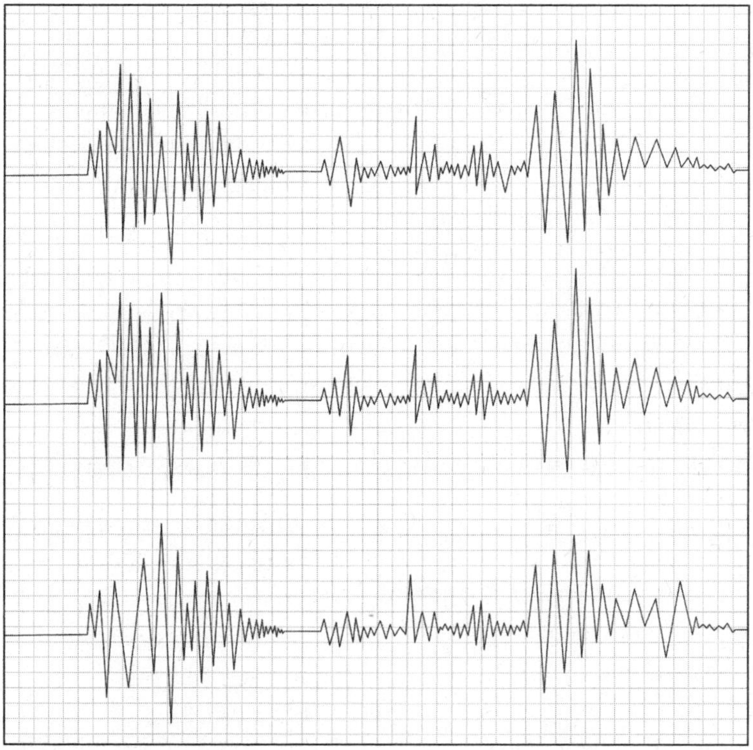

DID YOU KNOW? According to the American Psychological Association, polygraph tests could appear accurate because subjects who believe the tests work might confess or be anxious during questioning.

Political Crimes

Answer the questions to test your knowledge about political crimes.

1. ______ refers to the conduct of offering or receiving money or goods to obtain some kind of benefit.
2. ______ peddling involves the improper use of position of power to obtain benefits, either for oneself or for others.
3. Which of the following qualifies as a political crime?
   a. Election fraud
   b. Abuse of office
   c. Treason
   d. All of the above
4. True or false: Treason is the only crime mentioned in the United States Constitution.
5. Why was former vice president Aaron Burr acquitted of all charges of treason?
   a. Because he had not overtly done anything, only planned it.
   b. Because he wasn't successful.
   c. Because he bribed the judge.
   d. Because he didn't show up to trial.
6. True or false: Political criminals may actually give other people money rather than stealing for their personal use.
7. What landmark public corruption investigation, which coincidentally shares its name with Tennessee's state song, led to new state ethics laws and the creation of an independent ethics commission in Tennessee?
   a. Memphis Shuffle
   b. Tennessee Waltz
   c. Nashville Swing
   d. Ashville Disco
8. True or false: The Watergate scandal marked the first time a U.S. cabinet official served jail time for a felony committed while in office.
9. ______ is conduct or speech that incites individuals to violently rebel against the authority of the government.
   a. Insurrection
   b. Sedition
   c. Terrorism
   d. Nepotism
10. Which of the following governments and groups were NOT involved in the Iran-Contra Affair?
   a. Nicaraguan rebels
   b. United States
   c. Costa Rica
   d. Iran

DID YOU KNOW? Rodney James Alcala was already a prolific serial killer when he appeared as Bachelor No. 1 on the 1978 TV show *The Dating Game*.

Labyrinth of Lies

See how quickly you can make your way through this labyrinth of dead ends and misdirection.

Types of Evidence

Find all the listed words in the grid of letters. Words can be found in any direction—horizontally, vertically, or diagonally. They can be either forward or backward.

W	T	Z	I	B	I	L	A	P	K	D	D	U	V	J	W	M	J	P	M	Z	Y	L
Q	J	S	Q	L	V	G	U	K	Y	T	T	S	Z	B	R	D	X	R	S	A	M	E
E	Y	E	W	I	T	N	E	S	S	N	R	C	L	L	F	O	O	T	A	G	E	Q
C	E	Y	S	Z	X	R	Z	C	I	Z	T	I	B	A	M	C	J	R	V	Q	V	S
R	X	O	D	E	V	V	G	R	M	E	Y	T	U	I	U	U	F	A	A	I	I	O
G	P	R	O	G	M	U	P	X	S	F	N	S	L	T	S	M	K	U	J	X	D	B
W	E	P	O	I	O	R	B	T	O	D	E	I	A	N	I	E	J	D	T	N	E	P
W	R	R	L	B	E	W	I	R	U	Y	E	L	C	A	G	N	E	I	U	O	O	I
K	T	S	B	G	P	M	E	Z	E	V	A	L	I	T	S	T	E	O	D	I	R	L
Q	Q	T	N	F	O	N	M	E	K	N	E	A	S	S	T	A	P	X	W	S	R	D
X	D	I	I	N	S	W	T	C	X	C	Q	B	Y	M	M	G	Q	F	L	S	L	K
V	F	B	Y	I	P	T	Z	A	Q	S	O	V	H	U	A	S	X	R	A	E	I	C
M	T	I	C	P	O	T	F	R	U	W	N	E	P	C	X	J	I	F	J	F	E	I
K	X	H	R	W	E	S	I	T	L	T	P	O	W	R	O	J	B	R	F	N	Z	U
C	K	X	Z	Z	J	A	Y	Y	J	D	Z	E	P	I	M	K	I	O	K	O	P	M
P	Q	E	X	A	H	S	G	I	R	G	B	E	Z	C	A	K	K	M	R	C	Y	J

Word Bank

alibi	blood	document	eyewitness	forensic	testimony
audio	circumstantial	exhibit	fingerprint	hair	trace
ballistics	confession	expert	footage	physical	video

'80s Crime

Answer the questions to test your knowledge about crimes that took place in the 1980s.

1. Why was John DeLorean, creator of the car made famous by the *Back to the Future* movie trilogy, arrested for a narcotics law violation but found not guilty?

2. Why did New York City residents call mugging victim Bernhard Goetz the "Subway Vigilante"?
   a. He started up a neighborhood watch group on the subway to fend off street crime.
   b. He shot his would-be muggers, four teenagers who blocked his exit from the number 2 train, and demanded $5.
   c. He beat up a pair of muggers who were trying to steal a woman's purse.
   d. He stole from subway muggers.

3. True or false: The Billionaire Boys Club, a Ponzi scheme that swindled the fortunes of wealthy young men, got bilked itself by a shady "investor."

4. Which heavy metal band frontman was charged with attempted murder after he attacked his wife in a drunken state with the intention of killing her?

5. True or false: Despite a taped confession and fingerprint match, the state won't prosecute Michelle Schofield's real murderer because he is unreliable.

6. The murders of Shannon Lloyd in 1987 and Renee Cuevas in 1989 were solved two decades later with:
   a. A taped confession
   b. Eyewitness testimony
   c. Genetic genealogy
   d. Fingerprints

7. The 1980s saw a major surge in anti-abduction activism, including:
   a. The rise of the National Center for Missing and Exploited Children
   b. Mass-produced postcards and pictures printed on milk cartons to draw attention to cases
   c. Billboards to seek information
   d. All of the above

8. What member of the Gambino crime family was known as "The Dapper Don" for his taste in expensive clothes and personality with the media?

9. Nick De Noia, an Emmy Award–winning television producer and choreographer, was working as creative director of which famous nightclub show in New York City when he was murdered?

Futoshiki

Fill in the blank squares so that each of the numbers 1 through 4 appears exactly once in each row and column and the relationships between the squares meet the constraints of the inequality symbols.

#9

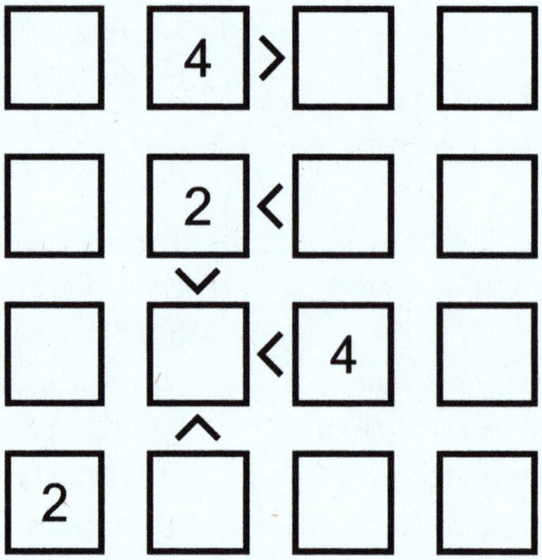

#10

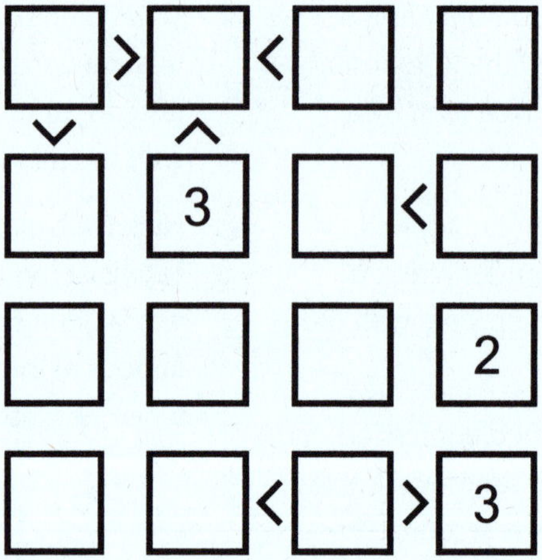

Kakuro #5

Fill in the blank squares with a number from 1 to 9 so that they add up to the given clues in the black, prefilled squares. Numbers cannot repeat in any across or down "run" of numbers. For a refresher on how to solve kakuro puzzles, see page 11.

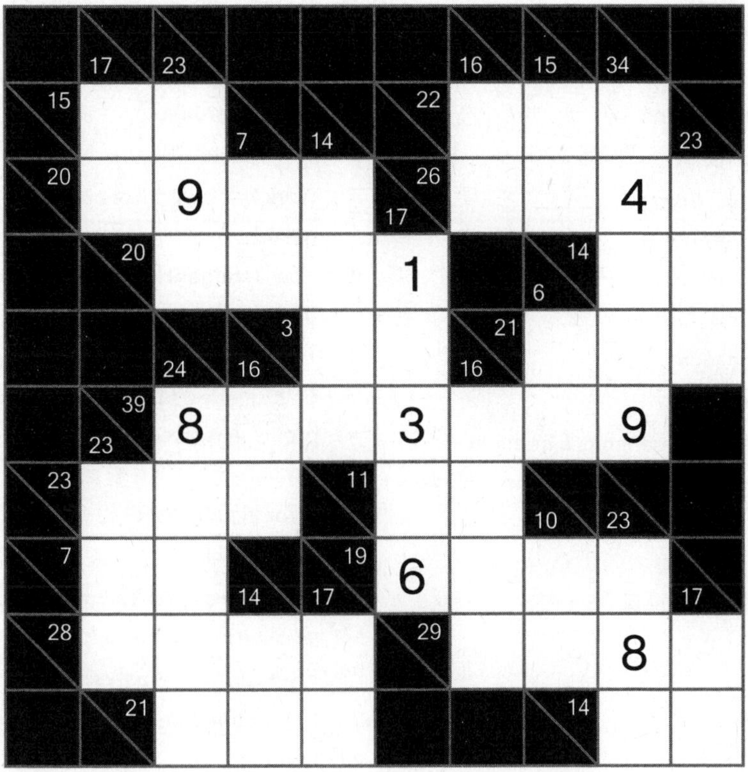

DID YOU KNOW? In 1998, MIT and Quaker Oats Co. were ordered to pay $1.85 million to young boys who underwent experiments in the '40s and '50s that tested how their bodies absorbed nutrients from cereal and milk laced with radioactive iron and calcium.

Criminal Profiling

Across

3. The injured party in a crime
8. First modern case to use profiling occurred in this northwest state
9. Careful study
11. Violent Criminal Apprehension Program, for short
13. Study of injured parties
14. Information bank
17. Mindhunter John Edward ______
20. The Roadside Strangler's ______ was to strangle women between the ages of 14 and 25
21. A suspect's makeup
22. ______-based case
25. The way an offender commits a crime is known as their ______ ______ (two words)
26. Oversight
28. Skill
30. Bloodhound, for example

Down

1. Federal Bureau of Investigation, for short
2. John Douglas's name for the 12 FBI profilers who worked with him on cases (two words)
4. Where evidence is gathered (two words)
5. ______ in traits, ages, habits, and other demographic details help construct accurate criminal profiles
6. Singled out
7. Work backward from an observed crime (two words)
10. How J. Edgar Hoover described the study of the criminal mind
12. The study of one's mind and behavior
15. This killer's case was the first time a victim profile was used to warn the public (two words)
16. Error in judgment
18. ______ killers
19. The case of this New York City serial killer gave birth to criminal profiling (two words)
23. FBI's ______ Analysis Unit
24. Unidentified person of interest, abbr.
27. Restrict
29. Working hypothesis

1
2
3
4
5
6
7
8
9
10
11
12
13
14
15
16
17
18
19
20
21
22
23
24
25
26
27
28
29
30

Rogues' Gallery

The first of its kind, this development from the 1840s helped identify prisoners in Belgium who committed crimes after their sentences ended. Solve this acrostic to find out what it is.

1. Infiltrator
2. Carried out in secret
3. Bet the house
4. Import secretly
5. Take over by force
6. Type of citrus
7. Match game

1									
2									
3									
4									
5									
6									
7									

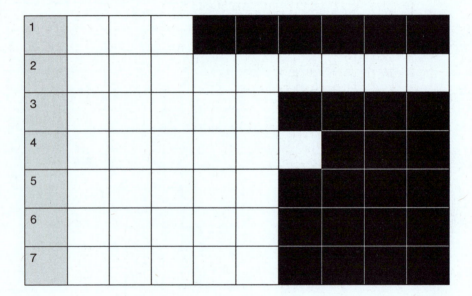

DID YOU KNOW? Bertillonage, a rigorous process devised by the French criminologist Alphonse Bertillon that procured several body measurements, was the first scientific method for identifying repeat criminals.

Sudoku #10

Fill in the remaining squares so that each of the numbers 1 through 9 appears exactly once in each row, column, and block.

			3		2		7	6
7		2				9		
9	3	6	5			8	4	2
		4				6	5	
	9						2	8
					5			
	8	7		3			6	
4	6			8	7		3	9
3	1		6			2	8	7

Criminal Investigative Analysis

Answer the questions to test your knowledge about criminal profiling.

1. Name at least one step in the FBI's system of criminal profiling.

2. What is often considered the first-ever criminal profile?
   a. Metropolitan Police surgeon Thomas Bond's report about Jack the Ripper
   b. Psychiatrist James Brussel's profile of New York City's Mad Bomber
   c. John Douglas's profile of serial killer Robert Hansen
   d. John Douglas's profile of Atlanta murderer Wayne Williams

3. Who is the first modern criminal profiler?
   a. Thomas Bond
   b. James Brussel
   c. John Douglas
   d. Robert Ressler

4. What year was the National Center for the Analysis of Violent Crime (NCAVC) created?
   a. 1956
   b. 1968
   c. 1975
   d. 1984

5. Which case did profiling work lead to a completely different conclusion from the police, district attorney, and FBI?
   a. JonBenet Ramsey
   b. Meredith Kercher
   c. West Memphis Three
   d. Kathleen Peterson

6. What breakthrough idea did profiler Roy Hazelwood contribute to the process?
   a. Proposing strategies for identifying, apprehending, and questioning the accused.
   b. Classifying serial homicide crime scenes according to an organized/disorganized dichotomy.
   c. Narrowing the list of subjects and implementing strategies that are likely to lead to arrest.
   d. Fine-tuning the computerized algorithms used by the profiling system to increase accuracy in the future.

7. True or false: An offender's MO is a learned behavior that is dynamic and malleable.

8. Which of these descriptions was NOT part of James Brussel's profile of the Mad Bomber?
   a. Foreign
   b. In his 50s
   c. Drove a pickup truck
   d. Had a vendetta against Con Edison

9. How many serial murderers were interviewed to develop theories and categories of different types of offenders?
   a. 5
   b. 12
   c. 36
   d. 50

Magic Square

Using the numbers 1 through 16, fill in the empty squares so that each row, column, and diagonal adds up to 34. Each number can be used only once.

#11

	10		
3			14
9	5		
16			1

#12

		12	
5		8	
	3	13	
		1	2

Undercover Investigations

Using the words listed in the word bank, fill in the grid.

Word Bank

agent	backstop	dead drop	operation	surveillance
alias	clandestine	deep cover	shadowing	target
asset	covert	infiltrate	sting	wiretap

Anna "Delvey" Sorokin

Unscramble the words that tell the story of Anna Delvey.

1. nco attsir

___

2. efak ressehi

___

3. edufdra

___

4. amsremc

___

5. yfslafi

___

6. icoestila

___

7. tasr lucb

___

8. isrekr lsidan

___

DID YOU KNOW? The FBI's Most Wanted list originated from a journalist asking the FBI for the names and descriptions of the "toughest guys" they wanted to capture.

’90s Crime

Answer the questions to test your knowledge about crimes that took place in the 1990s.

1. Which rock band frontman’s actions to seize a fan’s camera during a concert caused a violent riot that injured 65 people and resulted in property damage worth about $200,000?
   a. Axl Rose
   b. Steven Tyler
   c. Vince Neil
   d. Bret Michaels
2. Why did Jonathan Schmitz kill Scott Amedure a few days after they appeared together on the *Jenny Jones* talk show?
   a. Scott revealed he was cheating with Jonathan’s girlfriend.
   b. Scott revealed he had a crush on Jonathan.
   c. Scott revealed he was the father of Jonathan’s girlfriend’s child.
   d. Scott revealed he was in a relationship with Jonathan’s mother.
3. True or false: Twenty-three-year-old singer Selena was murdered by her manager.
4. A pipe bomb was found under a bench in the Centennial Olympic Park during which Olympic Games?
   a. 1992 Barcelona, Spain, summer games
   b. 1994 Lillehammer, Norway, winter games
   c. 1996 Atlanta, Georgia, summer games
   d. 1998 Nagano, Japan, winter games
5. True or false: Under the Violent Crime Control and Law Enforcement Act of 1994, which introduced the “three strikes and you’re out” rule, California’s prison population grew more than twice as fast as that of the state in the 1990s.
6. Which of the following is NOT a reason crime rate fell in the ’90s?
   a. Increased jail population
   b. The receding crack epidemic
   c. Legalization of abortion
   d. Gun control laws
7. Who is the “Long Island Lolita”?
8. What set off a three-day-long riot in Los Angeles in 1992?
   a. The acquittal of LAPD police officers after their use of excessive force to arrest Rodney King
   b. The acquittal of O. J. Simpson
   c. The murder of a young Black man by the LAPD
   d. A peaceful protest of police brutality that turned violent
9. Which *Saturday Night Live* cast member was murdered by his wife?
   a. Chris Farley
   b. Norm Macdonald
   c. Phil Hartman
   d. Peter Aykroyd

Shoe Prints

Examine the shoe prints to determine which set matches the one found at the scene of the crime.

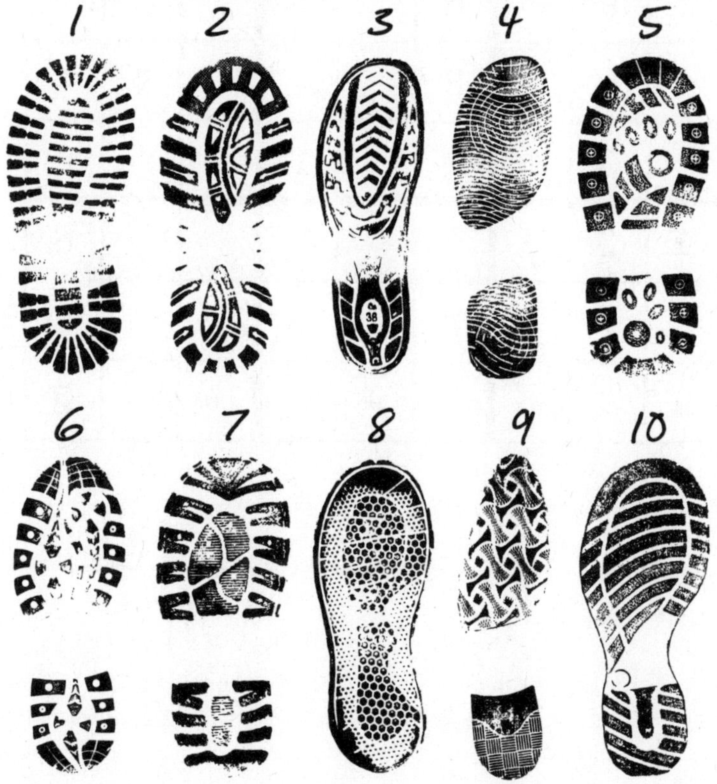

Sudoku #11

Fill in the remaining squares so that each of the numbers 1 through 9 appears exactly once in each row, column, and block.

7	6	8				3		1
	4		8	3		2	6	7
	1		4					
	9		6		4	7		
	5		3				1	4
	3				2			8
1	2	5	9					6
3	7		2		6	8		5
9				4				2

DID YOU KNOW? Lighthorse, the mounted police force that served and protected the citizens of the Chickasaw, Choctaw, Cherokee, Muscogee, and Seminole Nations in the 1800s, was named after General Henry "Lighthorse Harry" Lee.

A Dead End

There's only one way out among all these dead ends—can you find it?

Ransom Letter from Adolph Coors III's Kidnapper

Decode the following to reveal the ransom letter sent by the kidnapper. For a refresher on solving cryptograms, see page 9.

A	B	C	D	E	F	G	H	I	J	K	L	M
				2								
N	**O**	**P**	**Q**	**R**	**S**	**T**	**U**	**V**	**W**	**X**	**Y**	**Z**
				18								

7 18(R) 19 . 13 9 9 18(R) 19 : 15 9 14 18(R)

11 14 19 6 23 16 4 11 23 19 6 2(E) 2(E) 16

22 1 4 16 23 21 21 2(E) 4 . 11 1 19 13 23 18(R)

1 19 6 15 12 14 18(R) 22 2(E) 15 13 18(R) 2(E) 2(E) 22 .

13 23 20 20 12 11 2(E) 21 9 20 1 13 2(E) 9 18(R)

10 . 6 . 1 . : 11 2(E) 4 1 2(E) 19 .

[13][9][9][21][E 2][R 18][23][12][E 2]: [11][E 2] [20][1][24][E 2][19].

[R 18][23][16][19][9][7]: $200,000 [1][16]

[12][E 2][16][19] [23][16][4] $300,000 [1][16]

[12][26][E 2][16][12][1][E 2][19]. [12][11][E 2][R 18][E 2] [26][1][20][20]

[6][E 2] [16][9] [16][E 2][8][9][12][1][23][12][1][16][8].

[6][1][20][20][19]: [14][19][E 2][4] /

[16][9][16]—[13][9][16][19][E 2][13][14][12][1][24][E 2] /

[14][16][R 18][E 2][13][9][R 18][4][E 2][4] /

[14][16][7][23][R 18][22][E 2][4]. [26][23][R 18][16][1][16][8]:

[26][E 2] [26][1][20][20] [22][16][9][26] [1][10] [15][9][14]

[13][23][20][20] [12][11][E 2] [21][9][20][1][13][E 2] [9][R 18]

[R 18][E 2][13][9][R 18][4] [12][11][E 2]

[19][E 2][R 18][1][23][20] [16][14][7][6][E 2][R 18][19].

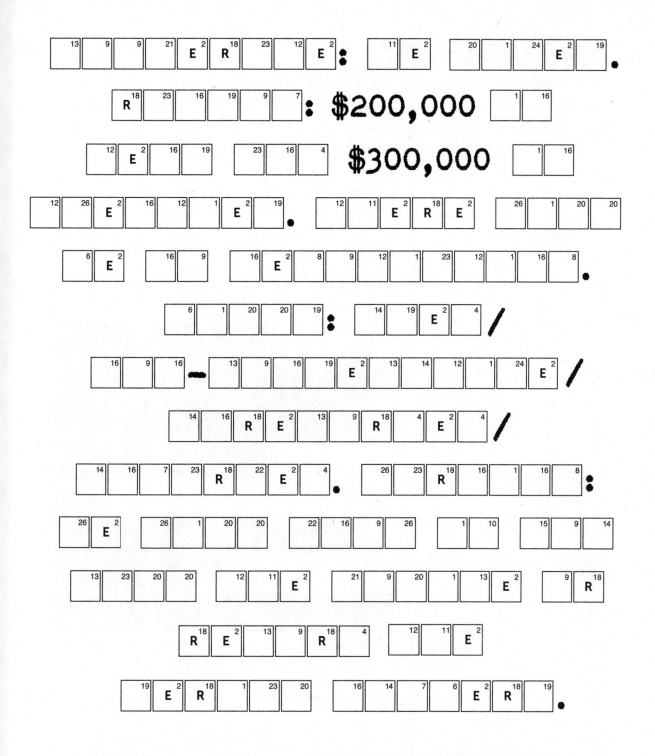

Spill the Beans

WikiLeaks volunteer Sigurdur "Siggi" Thordarson, Communist Party member Harvey Matusow, Anonymous hacker Sabu, to name a few. Solve the acrostic to find out what they have in common.

1. Presumed at trial
2. Duke or Earl
3. Grand larceny, for example
4. Something left out
5. Coined by the Employers' Association of Chicago in 1927 about the influence of organized crime in the Teamsters Union
6. Nikola Tesla had an eidetic one
7. Driver of the getaway car, for example
8. From dusk to dawn
9. When FBI wants to liven up an unproductive bugged conversation

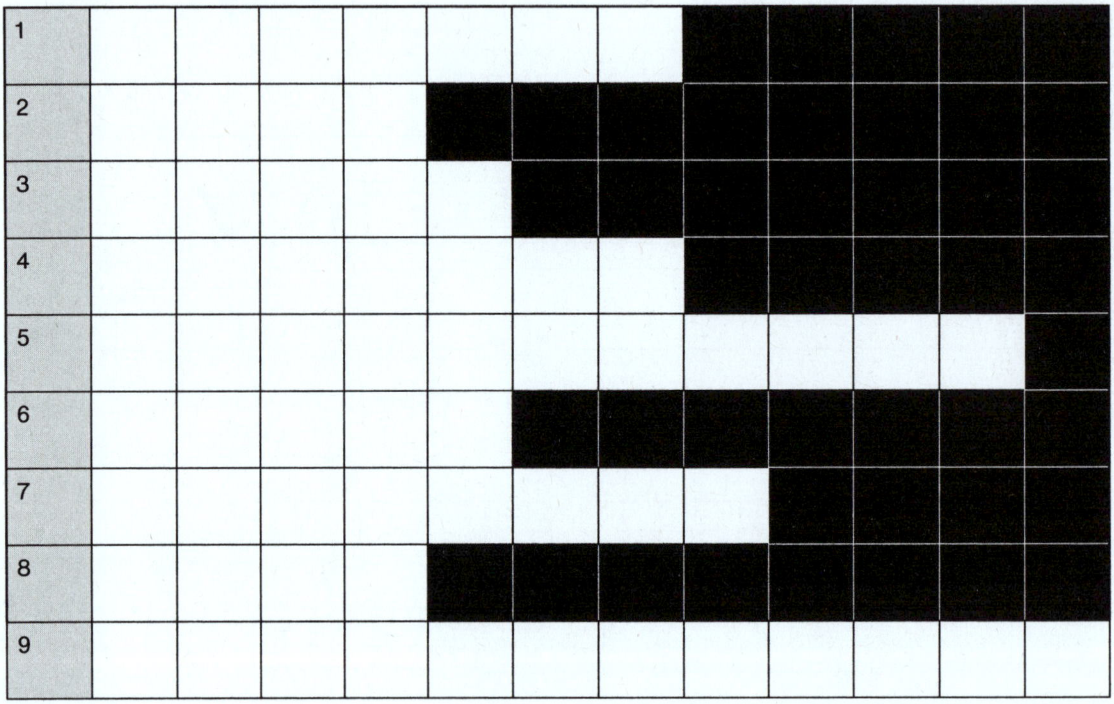

’00s Crime

Answer the questions to test your knowledge about crimes that took place in the 2000s.

1. Whose business’s wealth management arm was actually a multibillion-dollar Ponzi scheme?

2. Where were British couple Kate and Gerry McCann vacationing when their three-year-old daughter, Madeleine, vanished?
   a. Portugal
   b. California
   c. Spain
   d. Mexico

3. Executives of which company used fraudulent accounting practices and inaccurate financial reporting to cover up debts and failed ventures, leading to bankruptcy and employees losing their pensions and 401(k)s?
   a. Bank of America
   b. ExxonMobile
   c. Enron
   d. BP

4. What item did the Washington, DC, Beltway Snipers leave at some of the shooting sites in October 2002?
   a. A raven’s feather
   b. A tarot “Death” card
   c. A saint prayer card
   d. A book of poems

5. True or false: The Texas Seven, seven convicts who broke out of a South Texas maximum-security prison, fled to Colorado, where they lived as “Christian missionaries.”

6. Which home-living expert was sentenced to five months in prison for her role in an insider trading scandal?

7. Vickie Dawn Jackson, the “Angel of Death,” was known for injecting her elderly patients, including her husband’s grandfather, with mivacurium chloride, which stops patients’ ______.

8. Instead of physical mementos of his victims, serial killer Maury Travis kept ______, which were so disturbing that Police Chief Joe Mokwa arranged psychological counseling services for the deputies who viewed them.
   a. Sketches of his victims mid-torture
   b. Video recordings of him torturing his victims
   c. Photographs of his victims throughout the torture process
   d. Paintings of his dead victims

9. Which Louisiana city had two serial killers operating at the same time?
   a. Monroe
   b. Baton Rouge
   c. New Orleans
   d. Kentwood

10. True or false: Scott Kimball went on a killing spree while serving as an FBI informant.

Tracking a Killer

Track down the killer through their maze of lies.

Pay the Piper

List all the words you can make from the letters in PUNISHMENT.

Home, Sweet—Oh!

Answer the questions to test your knowledge about murder houses.

1. On June 10, 1912, someone entered a home in Villisca, Iowa, and murdered all eight of its occupants—the Moore family and two of the children's friends—with what weapon?
   a. A butcher knife
   b. An axe
   c. A rifle
   d. A baseball bat

2. What name did Ronald DeFeo Sr. give to his family's new home, which would eventually be known as the Amityville Horror House?
   a. High Hopes
   b. New Beginnings
   c. Fresh Start
   d. The Haven

3. Taliesin, architect Frank Lloyd Wright's Wisconsin residence with his mistress, was the site of a brutal murder, where a handyman attacked Wright's mistress and her children with a hatchet and then ______.
   a. Killed himself
   b. Buried their bodies in the garden
   c. Ran off
   d. Set the house on fire

4. True or false: A husband and wife used personal "lonely hearts" ads to lure women to their home in Germany, dubbed the Höxter Horror House, to torture them.

5. How were the crimes of UK serial killer Dennis Nilsen uncovered?
   a. One of his victims got away and led the police back to Nilsen's apartment.
   b. A neighbor called in a welfare check when she hadn't seen him for a week.
   c. He turned himself in.
   d. The neighbors in his apartment building complained of blocked drains—which were caused by human remains.

6. Which movie was NOT filmed at the Beverly Hills Greystone Mansion, the site of the murder of Ned Doheny, son of oil tycoon Edward L. Doheny?
   a. *The Witches of Eastwick*
   b. *Eraserhead*
   c. *Clueless*
   d. *Flowers in the Attic*

7. True or false: The Wonderland murders were not reported right away because neighbors assumed the screams they heard were from a party the residents—a drug-dealing gang—were having.

8. Two ex-convicts were looking for ______ when they broke into Herb and Bonnie Clutter's house in Holcomb, Kansas.

9. True or false: Lizzie Borden was convicted of killing her parents with an axe in their Fall River, Massachusetts, home.

Kakuro #6

Fill in the blank squares with a number from 1 to 9 so that they add up to the given clues in the black, prefilled squares. Numbers cannot repeat in any across or down "run" of numbers. For a refresher on how to solve kakuro puzzles, see page 11.

DID YOU KNOW? The dictograph was originally designed as a communications system but became one of the earliest electric eavesdropping devices, used by both police and private investigators.

Cold Cases Cracked

The unknown victims in these real cold cases have recently been named thanks to advances in DNA technology and the introduction of genetic genealogy research. Can you match up the monikers to the victims' names, the year they died, and where their bodies were found? For a refresher on how to solve a logic grid puzzle, see page 10.

CLUES

1. Ruth Marie Terry's case occurred in 1974 in Provincetown, Massachusetts.
2. The Bear Brook murders happened either in 1960 or 1985.
3. The 1948 case, which was the Somerton Man case, did not occur in Philadelphia, but it did involve Carl "Charles" Webb.
4. Sharon Lee Gallegos, whose case occurred in 1960, is either the Boy in the Box or the victim in the Arizona case.
5. The case in Australia did not happen in 1960, but it did involve the Somerton Man.
6. Joseph Augustus Zarelli's case, which was not the Bear Brook murders case, occurred in either 1957 or in New Hampshire.
7. The Lady of the Dunes case did not happen in Arizona but did occur in 1974.
8. The Boy in the Box case occurred in 1957.
9. The Bear Brook murders took place in New Hampshire.

		LOCATION					VICTIM					YEAR				
		Australia	Philadelphia	Provincetown, MA	Arizona	New Hampshire	Carl "Charles" Webb	Ruth Marie Terry	Sharon Lee Gallegos	Joseph Augustus Zarelli	Marlyse Elizabeth Honeychurch	1948	1957	1960	1974	1985
MONIKER	Lady of the Dunes															
	Bear Brook murders															
	Somerton Man															
	Boy in the Box															
	Little Miss Nobody															
YEAR	1948															
	1957															
	1960															
	1974															
	1985															
VICTIM	Carl "Charles" Webb															
	Ruth Marie Terry															
	Sharon Lee Gallegos															
	Joseph Augustus Zarelli															
	Marlyse Elizabeth Honeychurch															

Sudoku #12

Fill in the remaining squares so that each of the numbers 1 through 9 appears exactly once in each row, column, and block.

	5	8	4	7		9	6	
			1				5	8
6	1			5	8	4	7	2
7	2		5		4			
	9			3		8		
		4	9		7			
						7		
4	8	2						6
1					3		9	

Futoshiki

Fill in the blank squares so that each of the numbers 1 through 4 appears exactly once in each row and column and the relationships between the squares meet the constraints of the inequality symbols.

#11

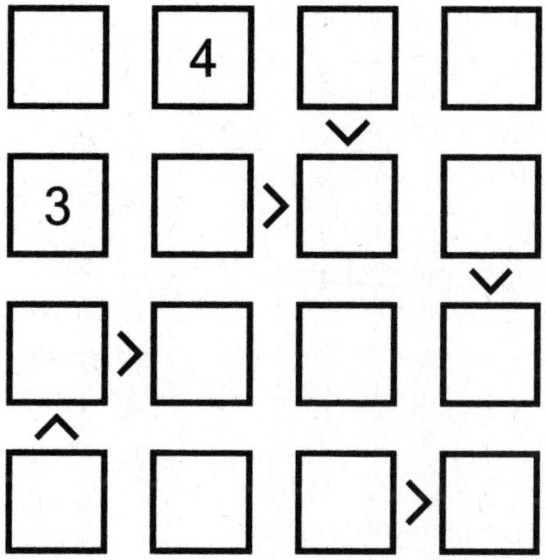

#12

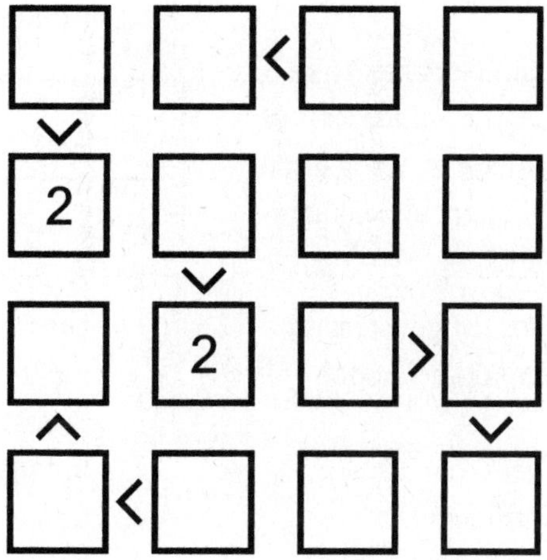

All or Nothing

Answer the questions to test your knowledge about casino heists.

1. True or false: New Zealand businessman James Manning won $33 million playing blackjack at the Melbourne, Australia, Crown Casino with the help of breached security cameras and card signaling, but he didn't cash out all his winnings.

2. How did the MIT Blackjack Team win tens of millions of dollars from casinos around the world?
   a. Distracting the dealer to move chips
   b. Card counting
   c. Switching cards
   d. Card marking

3. Twelve years after Heather Tallchief's convicted murderer boyfriend instructed her to steal ______ carrying $3 million meant for Las Vegas casino ATMs, she turned herself in.

4. True or false: A trio of gamblers had to return $1.7 million to the London Ritz Casino, which they'd won in roulette by using laser scanners and microcomputers to calculate where the ball would land.

5. How was Rolando Ramos caught stealing $1.5 million from his employer, Soboba Casino?
   a. At least ten employees saw his face.
   b. He left behind his business card.
   c. He ran into his boss.
   d. He went back to the scene of the crime.

6. Why did Anthony Carleo, who robbed the Bellagio and Suncoast casinos in Las Vegas, call himself the "Biker Bandit"?

7. True or false: in 1992, Stardust Casino cashier Bill Brennan walked out with $500,000 in cash and casino chips and was never caught.

8. On his ______ attempt at robbing Treasure Island, Reginald Johnson was finally captured.

9. How did Erik Gutierrez-Martinez steal over $1 million from Circa Hotel & Casino?
   a. He just walked in and demanded it.
   b. He posed as the owner of the casino and convinced a hotel employee to send him the money.
   c. He worked for the casino and took home small amounts every week.
   d. He hired someone.

10. Originally, Sabrina Eddy told officers that she took ten bricks of $50,000 each from the vault of Colorado's Monarch Casino because:
    a. A casino boss ordered her to bring the cash to an attorney in a hospital parking lot.
    b. A voice in her head told her to take out the money and donate it to a charity.
    c. She was borrowing it to help a friend and planned on putting it back.
    d. She was being threatened by associates of her deceased husband.

Black Sox Scandal

Find all the listed words in the grid of letters. Words can be found in any direction—horizontally, vertically, or diagonally. They can be either forward or backward.

Y	S	N	R	G	F	K	W	O	R	H	T	D	L	I	W	M	N	Z	M	C	Q	G
P	E	A	C	A	M	F	F	W	K	L	J	Q	E	D	V	O	S	I	M	K	G	M
W	M	V	R	O	E	S	E	F	L	P	Z	L	Z	K	I	R	E	S	U	L	L	W
L	E	I	B	Z	O	K	Z	A	N	Y	E	M	A	G	N	W	O	R	H	T	F	J
R	H	L	S	U	J	R	B	K	T	S	S	B	Y	Q	W	X	C	E	I	S	H	B
E	C	L	O	L	S	E	Z	V	X	O	S	E	T	I	H	W	F	W	P	V	A	Y
D	S	U	I	Q	S	K	E	I	T	U	O	N	E	M	T	H	G	I	E	L	W	G
S	A	S	W	A	E	E	O	D	J	W	J	R	C	H	I	C	A	G	O	L	E	A
C	N	T	B	L	L	K	C	E	L	C	H	I	C	K	G	A	N	D	I	L	W	M
Z	D	R	C	D	E	L	I	B	E	R	A	T	E	E	R	R	O	R	D	P	C	B
S	E	O	Q	R	O	W	O	R	L	D	S	E	R	I	E	S	T	H	Y	U	T	L
T	B	P	E	P	H	U	U	N	G	Y	W	S	J	B	X	J	C	R	P	R	P	E
J	T	S	P	B	S	Z	T	G	D	X	J	H	N	F	I	X	H	P	I	E	R	R
A	V	L	H	Q	C	Z	O	V	J	C	O	G	F	E	R	O	M	W	W	V	Y	T
E	F	E	S	U	S	P	I	C	I	O	U	S	P	L	A	Y	P	D	N	O	E	S
D	H	W	X	E	S	U	A	L	C	E	S	R	E	V	E	R	A	L	T	C	T	A

Word Bank

baseball	coverup	fix	reverse clause	Sport Sullivan	White Sox
Chicago	deliberate error	gambler	scheme	suspicious play	wild throw
Chick Gandil	Eight Men Out	Reds	Shoeless Joe	thrown game	World Series

Magic Square

Fill in the empty squares so that each row, column, and diagonal adds up to 75 (#13) and 45 (#14). Each number can be used only once.

#13

35		15
	5	40

#14

		12
	15	9
	3	

Crime Lab

Overnight, someone broke into the crime lab and disturbed a scientist's work area. There are 10 differences. Can you find them?

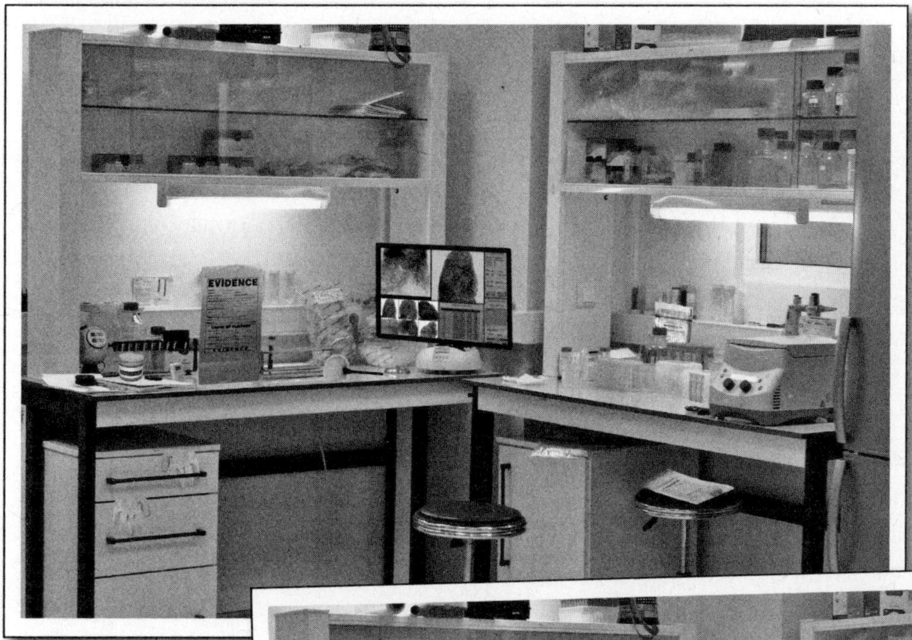

BEFORE

AFTER

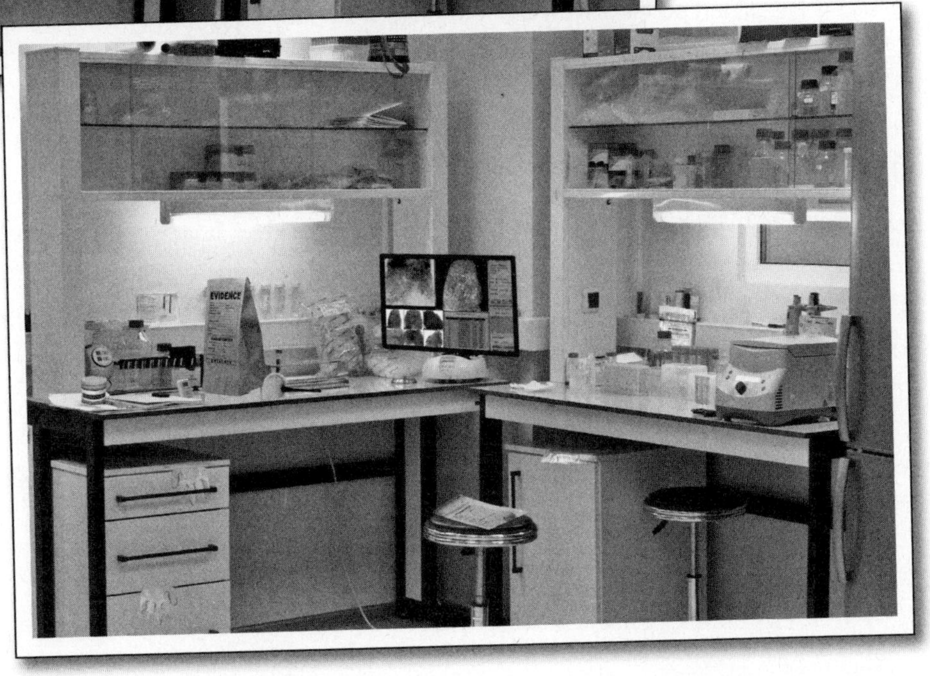

"You and I Are Going to Make a Lot of Money Together"

Answer the questions to test your knowledge about con artists.

1. When was the term "con man" first coined?
   a. 1849
   b. 1913
   c. 1922
   d. 1938
2. How did William Thompson, the first con man, scam complete strangers on the streets of New York City?
   a. He pretended he had a twisted ankle and stole their wallets while they helped him cross the street.
   b. He told them he was psychic and they paid for a reading.
   c. He gained people's trust quickly and convinced them to hand over their watches.
   d. He convinced people that he was a doctor and they paid him for his advice.
3. Sylvia Browne was a celebrity ______ with a big following whose accuracy with unsolved cases was 0 percent.
4. Spokesman for the US Drug Enforcement Administration Garrison Courtney convinced military and intelligence officials that he was ______.
   a. FBI
   b. A spy
   c. CSI
   d. A high-ranking military officer
5. True or false: David Hampton told people he was Sidney Poitier's son so that the Park Plaza staff would offer him a free limousine ride to Studio 54.
6. Which director did Alan Conway, an English con man, impersonate?
   a. Steven Spielberg
   b. James Cameron
   c. Stanley Kubrick
   d. George Lucas
7. Which of the following did the Great Imposter Ferdinand Waldo Demara NOT claim to be?
   a. Navy doctor
   b. A TV producer
   c. Biologist
   d. Monk
8. What personality traits make up the dark triad, which can predispose people to becoming con artists?
   a. Narcissism
   b. Psychopathy
   c. Ambition
   d. Machiavellianism
9. True or false: Con artists play to intelligence, not emotions.
10. What is the term "con man" short for?

Sudoku #13

Fill in the remaining squares so that each of the numbers 1 through 9 appears exactly once in each row, column, and block.

3						7		4
8	5	7	9		6	3		
		1		5		9		
				9		8	6	2
9					5			7
6		8	4	2			9	5
			5		4			
7	3	5	6		9			8
	6		2			5	7	

DID YOU KNOW? Fencing is the act of selling stolen property through a middleman or dealer in the criminal underworld.

Alcatraz Escapee's Letter

Decrypt this letter supposedly from John Anglin, one of three men who successfully escaped Alcatraz in 1962.

A	B	C	D	E	F	G	H	I	J	K	L	M
23				8							16	
N	**O**	**P**	**Q**	**R**	**S**	**T**	**U**	**V**	**W**	**X**	**Y**	**Z**
				25	4	17						

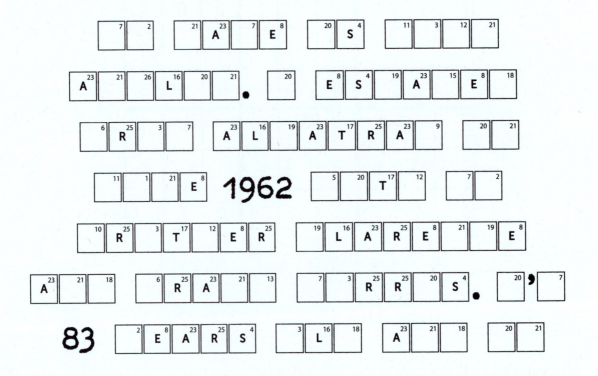

[7][2]   [21][A 23][7][E 8]   [20][S 4]   [11][3][12][21]

[A 23][21][26][L 16][20][21].   [20]   [E 8][S 4][19][A 23][15][E 8][18]

[6][R 25][3][7]   [A 23][L 16][19][A 23][T 17][R 25][A 23][9]   [20][21]

[11][1][21][E 8]   1962   [5][20][T 17][12]   [7][2]

[10][R 25][3][T 17][12][E 8][R 25]   [19][L 16][A 23][R 25][E 8][21][19][E 8]

[A 23][21][18]   [6][R 25][A 23][21][13]   [7][3][R 25][R 25][20][S 4].   [20]'[7]

83   [2][E 8][A 23][R 25][S 4]   [3][L 16][18]   [A 23][21][18]   [20][21]

_(10) A(23) _(18)   S(4) _(12) A(23) _(15) E(8).   _(20)   _(12) A(23) _(14) E(8)

_(19) A(23) _(21) _(19) E(8) R(25).   _(2) E(8) S(4)   _(5) E(8)   A(23) L(16) L(16)

_(7) A(23) _(18) E(8)   _(20) T(17)   T(17) _(12) A(23) T(17)   _(21) _(20) _(26) _(12) T(17)

_(10) _(1) T(17)   _(10) A(23) R(25) E(8) L(16) _(2)!   _(20) _(6)   _(2) _(3) _(1)

A(23) _(21) _(21) _(3) _(1) _(21) _(19) E(8)   _(3) _(21)   T(17) _(14)   T(17) _(12) A(23) T(17)   _(20)

_(5) _(20) L(16) L(16)   _(10) E(8)   _(15) R(25) _(3) _(7) _(20) S(4) E(8) _(18)   T(17) _(3)

_(6) _(20) R(25) S(4) T(17)   _(26) _(3)   T(17) _(3)   _(11) A(23) _(20) L(16)   _(6) _(3) R(25)

_(21) _(3)   _(7) _(3) R(25) E(8)   T(17) _(12) A(23) _(21)   A(23)   _(2) E(8) A(23) R(25)

A(23) _(21) _(18)   _(26) E(8) T(17)   _(7) E(8) _(18) _(20) _(19) A(23) L(16)

A(23) T(17) T(17) E(8) _(21) T(17) _(20) _(3) _(21),   _(20)   _(5) _(20) L(16) L(16)

_(5) R(25) _(20) T(17) E(8)   _(10) A(23) _(19) _(13)   T(17) _(3)   L(16) E(8) T(17)   _(2) _(3) _(1)

_(13) _(21) _(3) _(5)   E(8) _(24) A(23) _(19) T(17) L(16) _(2)   _(5) _(12) E(8) R(25) E(8)   _(20)

A(23) _(7).   T(17) _(12) _(20) S(4)   _(20) S(4)   _(21) _(3)   _(11) _(3) _(13) E(8).

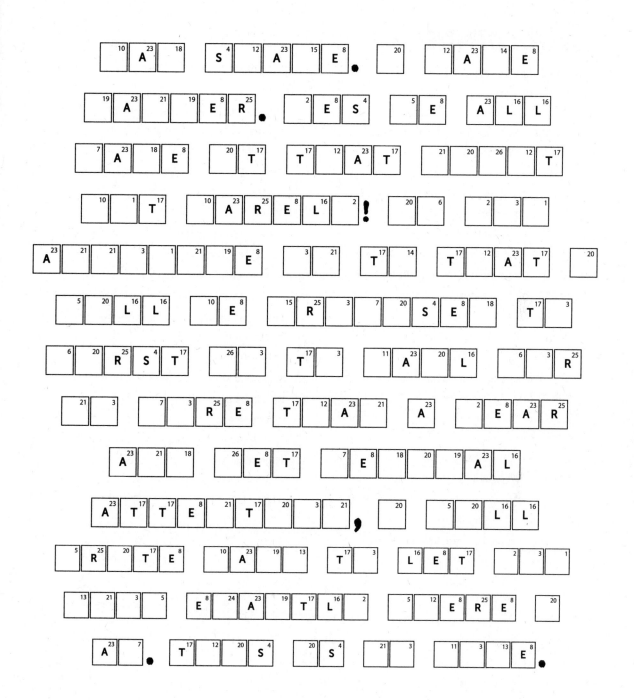

Cybercrime

Across

3. Manipulating people into divulging personal or confidential information is known as _______ engineering
7. Digital story
8. In 2014, North Korean hackers demanded _______ Pictures withdraw *The Interview*
9. Black-and-white twistable treat
11. A tool that cloaks devices, for short
13. Scams designed to trick you into giving sensitive information
15. _______ of data
17. Short, rude
19. Hidden sites (two words)
21. Sweet Bobby is the longest _______ case in the history of the internet
24. _______ phishing attacks are a more focused version
25. Malicious software, for short
26. A distinctive smell
28. Creator of the first computer virus in 1988
29. "Before" in old English
30. Business email compromise, for short

Down

1. Hackers attacking corporations or governments for political, competitive, or financial reasons is cyber _______
2. Two-_______ authentication
4. _______-day exploit, or none
5. Denial of _______ attack
6. Person, place, or thing
10. To encode information
12. Used to block cyberattacks
14. _______ Madison website data breach
16. Theft that involves stealing your personal information
18. Cybercriminal
20. Malicious software that demands money
22. Criminals pretending to be a legitimate business
23. A strong one can prevent data breaches
27. Flightless bird

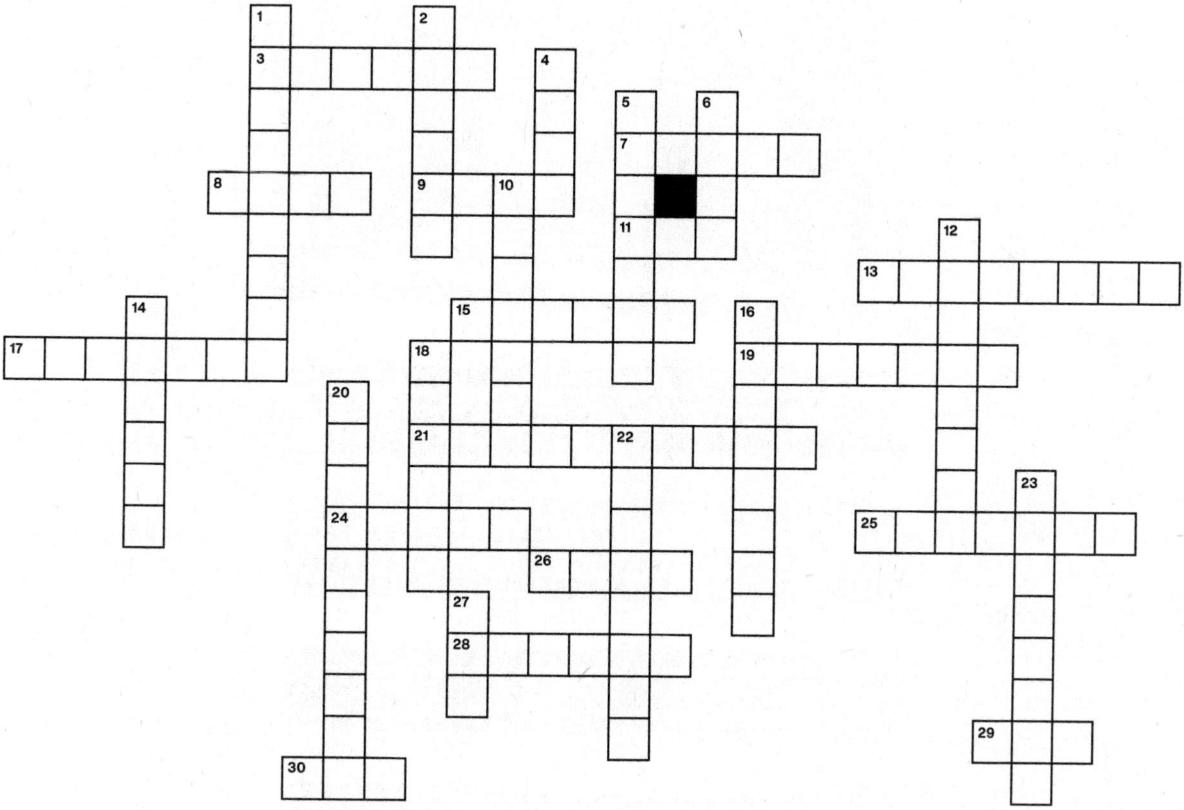

Tire Tracks Match

Find the matching tire print to determine which car was at the crime scene.

1

2

3

4

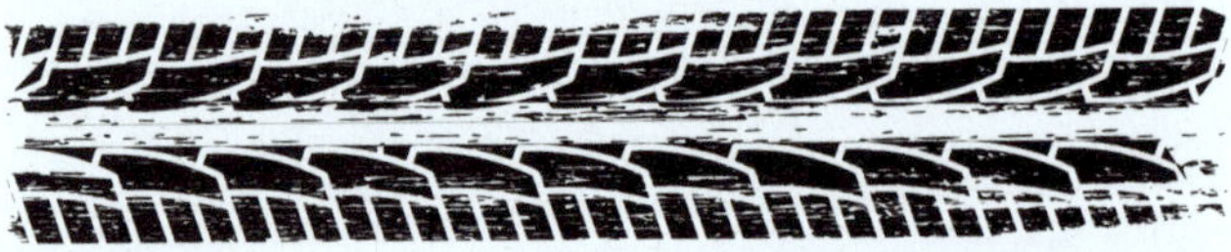

5

Covert Actions

Answer the questions to test your knowledge about espionage.

1. True or false: A spy is a professional intelligence officer.

2. A ______ is loyal to one side before being "turned" and transferring loyalties to the other side.

3. Which of the following is the correct order of the stages in the intelligence cycle?
   a. Planning, Collection, Processing, Analysis, Dissemination
   b. Dissemination, Planning, Collection, Processing, Analysis
   c. Planning, Collection, Analysis, Processing, Dissemination
   d. Collection, Dissemination, Processing, Analysis, Planning

4. What is espionage?
   a. The act of informing others you are a spy
   b. The act of catching a spy in the act
   c. The act of spying usually through illegal means
   d. The act of sharing information between two spies

5. What university were five students recruited from to spy for the Soviet Union in the 1930s?
   a. Oxford University
   b. Cambridge University
   c. MIT
   d. Harvard University

6. True or false: No spy in the Culper Spy Ring, which operated during the Revolutionary War, was ever unmasked.

7. Aldrich Hazen Ames, a 31-year veteran of the ______, was arrested on espionage charges after passing information to the KGB.

8. The UK Security Service, also known as MI5, was established in 1909 in response to fears of ______ espionage.
   a. Russian
   b. Chinese
   c. Japanese
   d. German

9. Xiaoqing Zheng was convicted of ______ espionage for conspiring to steal General Electric trade secrets to benefit China.

10. Which hotel chain recruited former employees of their competitor Starwood and used their confidential documents to copy Starwood's concepts?
   a. Hilton
   b. Marriott
   c. Ritz
   d. Wyndham

Futoshiki

Fill in the blank squares so that each of the numbers 1 through 4 appears exactly once in each row and column and the relationships between the squares meet the constraints of the inequality symbols.

#13

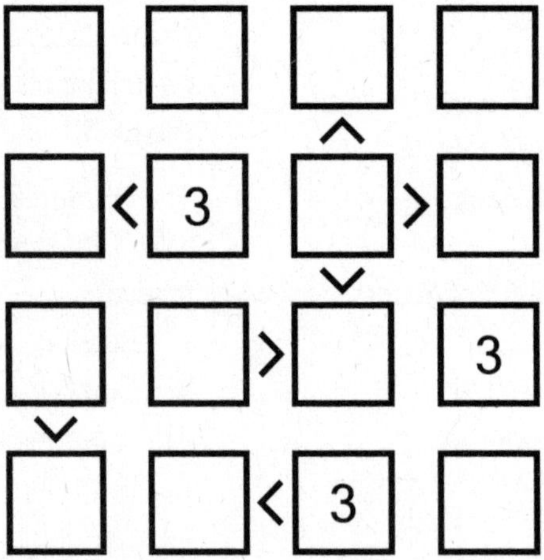

#14

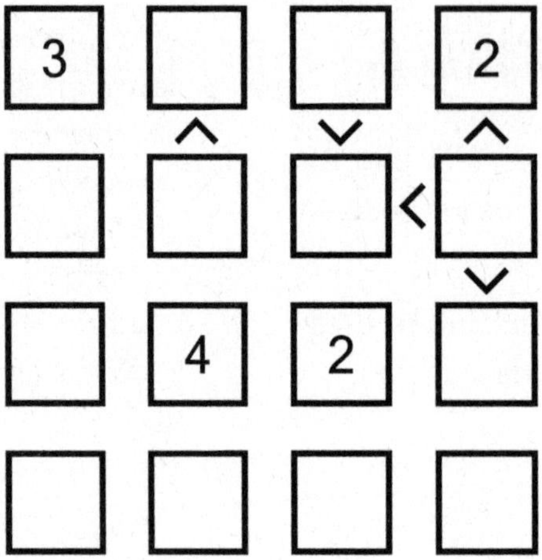

Stanford Prison Experiment

Using the words listed in the word bank, fill in the grid.

Word Bank

anonymous	guards	pushups	smock	volunteer
degradation	oppression	rebellion	study	warden
escape	psychology	simulation	sunglasses	Zimbardo

Billy the Kid

Unscramble the words that tell the story of Billy the Kid.

1. luatwo

2. prnaoh

3. nulgigesrn

4. het taegorrlsu

5. lttcea rrtlseu

6. ibkaerlja

7. lod twse

8. ofrt usenmr

Cops + Custody + Interrogation

What concept was created following a 1966 Supreme Court decision that found a defendant's Fifth and Sixth Amendment rights had been violated during their arrest and trial? Solve the acrostic to find out.

1. Utter chaos
2. Poison ______
3. Underlying cause
4. Court do-over
5. Drugs
6. Snoozefest
7. Defendant's hope
8. Threat, or theft of threat, by force
9. Martha's Vineyard, for ex.
10. Writing on the wall
11. Smoking is a bad one
12. Trade illegally
13. Established by written law

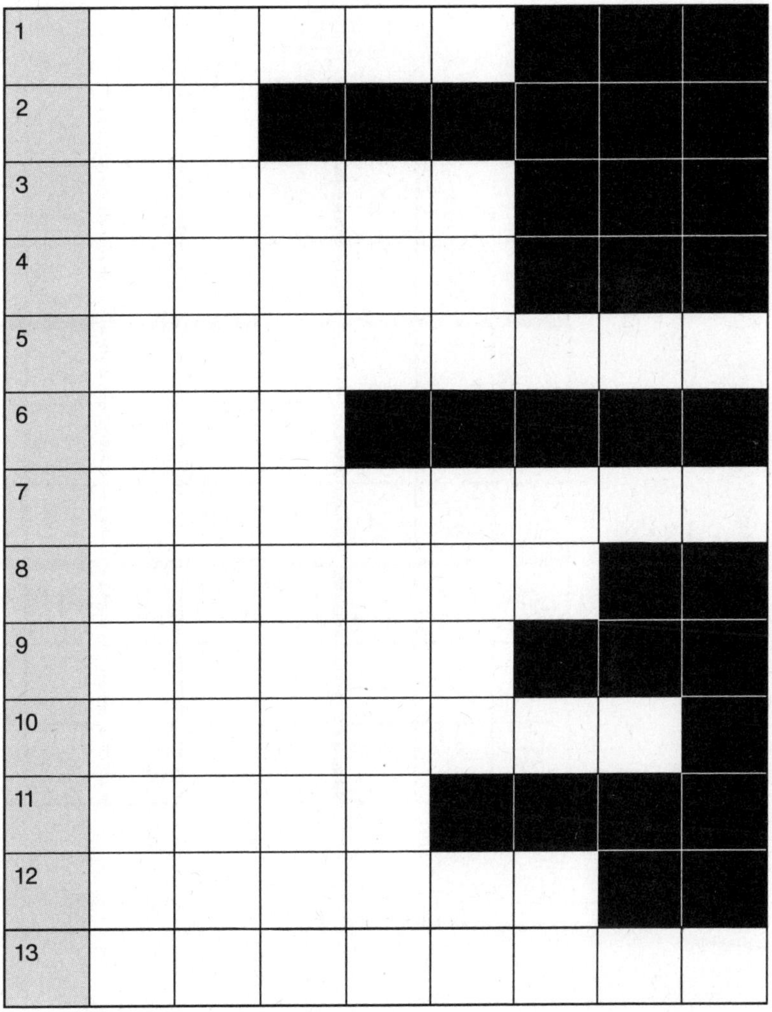

Sudoku #14

Fill in the remaining squares so that each of the numbers 1 through 9 appears exactly once in each row, column, and block.

1		5	4	3		2		8
		6		7		9		5
2	8							3
						3		
		9					5	
	2	3	6	9	7		8	
9				2	8	4	3	
8	7	4	3					
3					4	8		7

DID YOU KNOW? The Sesame Street Parent-Child Center was a program in federal prisons that dedicated space for kids who were visiting incarcerated loved ones.

John B. McLemore's Hedge Maze

While John B. McLemore's original hedge maze had 64 possible solutions, this one only has one—can you solve it?

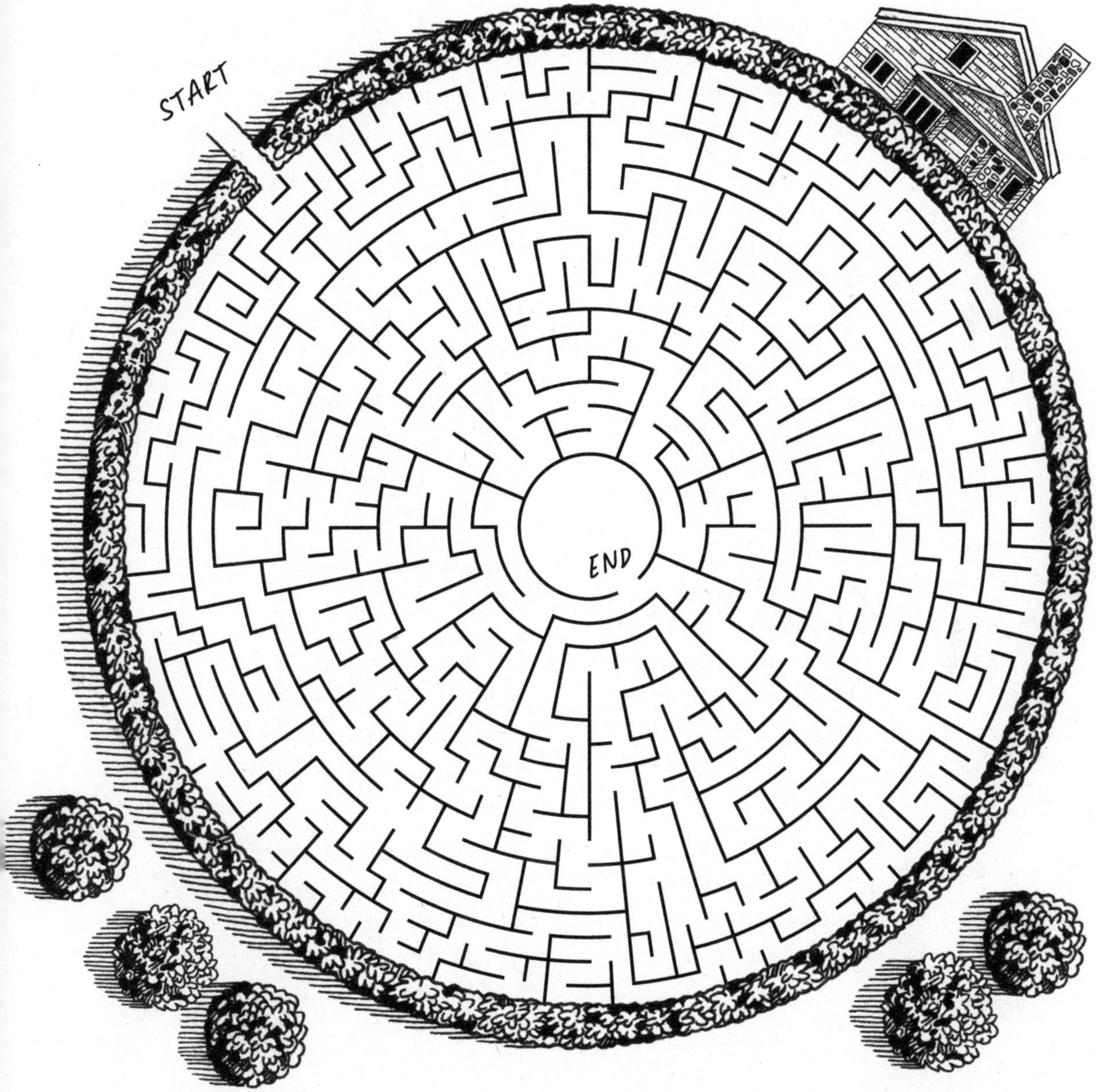

Is There a (Real) Doctor in the House?

Answer the questions to test your knowledge about medical crimes.

1. A nationwide network of stolen ______ involved a manager of the Harvard Medical School morgue, an employee of the Little Rock mortuary, and a convicted felon.

2. True or false: A surgeon at University Community Hospital amputated the wrong leg on a patient and only received a $10,000 fine and the loss of his medical license for six months.

3. Surgeons at Rhode Island Hospital in 2007 operated on the wrong side of patients' ______ three separate times.
   a. Brains
   b. Lungs
   c. Hearts
   d. Abdomens

4. The Lainz Angels of Death were four nurses in Vienna, Austria, who worked together to kill patients using morphine and later by ______.
   a. Smothering
   b. Strangling
   c. Drowning
   d. Starvation

5. Thrill Seekers, Power Oriented, Gain Motivated, and Missionary Killers are all categories of ______.

6. True or false: RaDonda Vaught is a nurse who was convicted in 2022 of negligent homicide for a patient's death when she forgot to give the patient her medication.

7. A Detroit-area doctor was convicted of writing prescriptions for millions of ______.
   a. Insulin injections
   b. Opioids
   c. Morphine injections
   d. Pain pills

8. What weight loss drug in the 1990s resulted in hundreds of cases of people developing heart valve abnormalities?
   a. Fen-Phen
   b. Leptin
   c. Ephedra
   d. Ozempic

9. True or false: Stephan Gevorkian, an alleged doctor practicing medicine without a certification in North Hollywood, California, was caught during an undercover operation in 2022.

10. Of the following celebrities, which one was NOT overprescribed by their doctors?
    a. Michael Jackson
    b. Anna Nicole Smith
    c. Chris Benoit
    d. Heath Ledger

Answer Key

Hook, Line, and Sinker

1. True
2. Scambaiter
3. b. Sunk the ship
4. Snake oil
5. c. He produced images with double exposures.
6. d. Planting artifacts so his team could get credit for discovering the oldest stone artifacts in Japan
7. Money mule
8. Her mother
9. a. People who had the surname Drake
10. d. All of the above

The Art of the Heist

Across

4. SMASH
5. ART CRIME TEAM
6. SPIDERMAN
9. VAN GOGH
11. BICYCLE
16. ALTARPIECE
18. TOILET
20. OLE
22. OSLO
24. FLORENCE
27. LEMON
28. IN
29. TEA BAGS

Down

1. RARE
2. GUARD
3. LATKES
4. STEWART
7. PROVENANCE
8. NAILS
10. SECURITY
12. PLURAL
13. APART
14. SAINT
15. PABLO
17. SKYLIGHT
19. ICE CREAM
21. ERGO
23. STENDHAL
25. CAPRIS
26. ARTNAP

Chicago Tylenol Murders

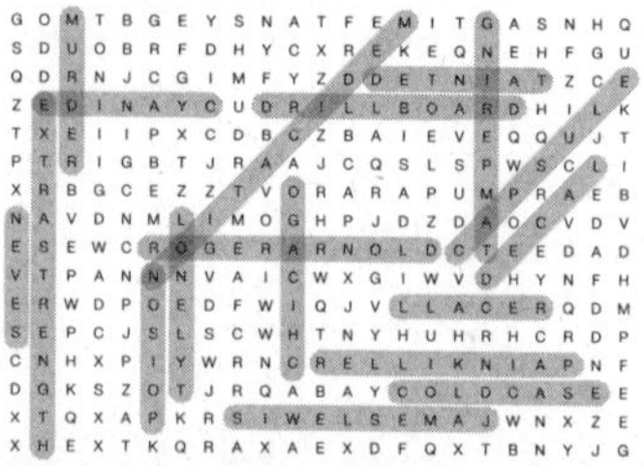

Check the Call Log

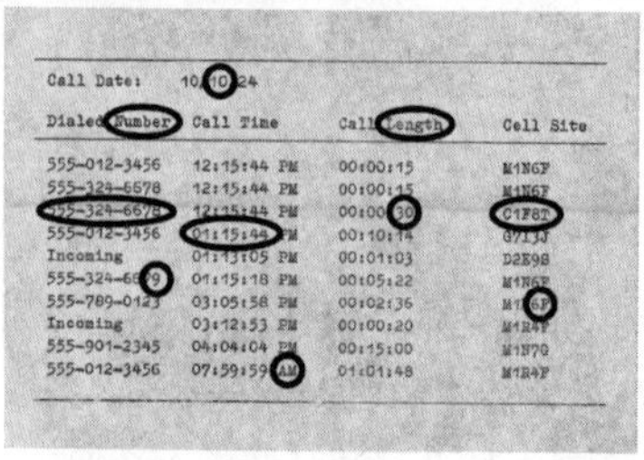

Call Date: 10/10/24

Dialed Number	Call Time	Call Length	Cell Site
555-012-3456	12:15:44 PM	00:00:15	M1N6F
555-324-6678	12:15:44 PM	00:00:15	M1N6F
555-324-6678	12:15:44 PM	00:00:30	C1F8T
555-012-3456	01:15:44 PM	00:10:14	G713J
Incoming	01:13:05 PM	00:01:03	D2E98
555-324-6679	01:15:18 PM	00:05:22	M1N6F
555-789-0123	03:05:58 PM	00:02:36	M1N6F
Incoming	03:12:53 PM	00:00:20	M1R4F
555-901-2345	04:04:04 PM	00:15:00	M1N7G
555-012-3456	07:59:59 AM	01:01:48	M1R4F

Where in the World?

1. Maple syrup
2. a. Norway
3. b. Dublin Castle
4. True
5. c. She made them into soaps and teacakes.
6. d. Ripperologist
7. d. All of the above
8. Bible
9. Philippines
10. b. High heels

Sudoku #1

1	6	4	5	9	7	3	8	2
2	7	8	1	4	3	6	9	5
5	9	3	8	2	6	7	1	4
9	2	5	6	7	1	4	3	8
7	8	6	4	3	9	2	5	1
3	4	1	2	8	5	9	6	7
6	5	7	9	1	2	8	4	3
4	3	9	7	5	8	1	2	6
8	1	2	3	6	4	5	7	9

Harvey's Casino Bomb Extortion Note

A	B	C	D	E	F	G	H	I	J	K	L	M
18	15	23	4	13	20	6	3	5	17	8	10	12

N	O	P	Q	R	S	T	U	V	W	X	Y	Z
21	14	24	11	1	9	7	19	22	25	2	16	26

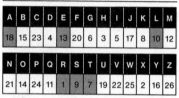

IF EXPLODED THIS BOMB CONTAINS ENOUGH TNT TO SEVERELY DAMAGE HARRAHS ACROSS THE STREET. THIS SHOULD GIVE YOU SOME IDEA OF THE AMOUNT OF TNT CONTAINED WITHIN THIS BOX. IT IS FULL OF TNT. IT IS OUR ADVICE TO CORDON OFF A MINIMUM OF TWELVE HUNDRED FEET RADIUS AND REMOVE ALL PEOPLE FROM THAT AREA.

Find the Footprint

Magic Square #1

4	3	8
9	5	1
2	7	6

Magic Square #2

8	1	6
3	5	7
4	9	2

The Art of Stealing

1. b. St. Patrick's Day
2. a. 1473
3. True
4. c. Thomas Jefferson
5. d. 13
6. a. Tinder
7. True
8. False. He was accused of insurance fraud.
9. b. Pablo Escobar
10. b. 5 to 10 percent

Sudoku #2

8	9	3	7	1	4	2	5	6
6	4	5	8	3	2	1	9	7
2	1	7	5	9	6	8	3	4
1	5	2	4	8	3	7	6	9
3	8	6	2	7	9	4	1	5
4	7	9	6	5	1	3	2	8
9	3	8	1	6	7	5	4	2
7	2	1	9	4	5	6	8	3
5	6	4	3	2	8	9	7	1

Black Dahlia

1. Los Angeles
2. mutilation
3. Elizabeth
4. unsolved
5. mannequin
6. murder
7. Hollywood
8. Glasgow smile

The Great Maple Syrup Heist

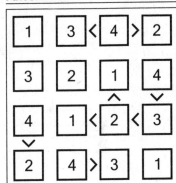

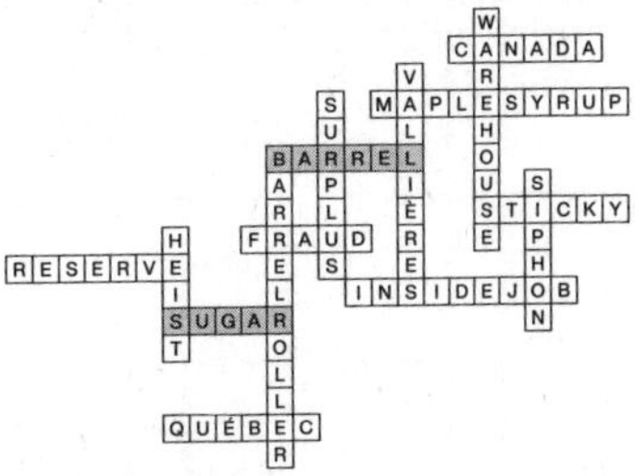

Crime Scene

Futoshiki #1

1		3	<	4	>	2
3		2		1		4
				^		v
4		1	<	2	<	3
v						
2		4	>	3		1

Futoshiki #2

3	4	1	2
4	2	3	1
2	1	4	3
1	3	2	4

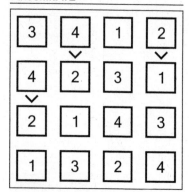

The CSI Effect

1. a. Grid, spiral, zone, linear
2. b. Forensic science
3. c. Complainant
4. False. It is a chronological record that tracks the movement of evidence from the crime scene to the courtroom.
5. Field notes
6. b. Create a hypothesis about the crime, which is then tested using the facts of the case.
7. True
8. Trace
9. a. Elimination prints
10. The effect of the exaggerated portrayal of forensic science on crime TV shows on the public's perception.

A Collector's Dream

1. Manslaughter
2. Universe
3. Robbery
4. Disorderly
5. Evidence
6. Requiem
7. Advocate
8. Blood
9. Investigation
10. Language
11. Indicate
12. Apron

Answer: Murderabilia

Kakuro #1

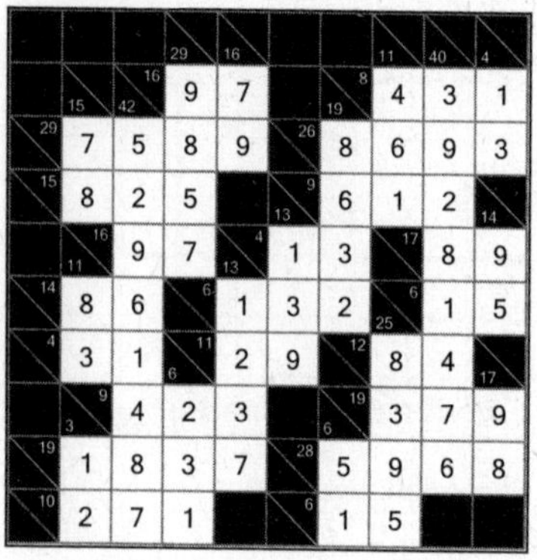

An Escape Route

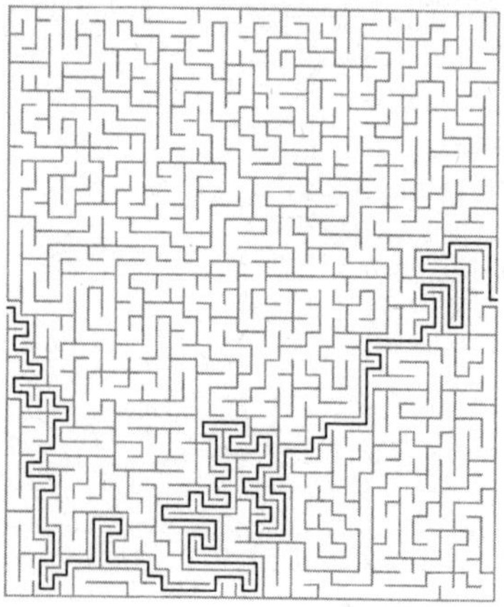

To Catch a Killer

1. d. Copycat killer
2. Bind, torture, kill
3. False. FBI Agent Robert Ressler is said to have coined the term "serial killer" in 1974. Though some argue that novelist Dorothy B. Hughes first used the term in her 1947 book *In a Lonely Place*.
4. c. Spray paint specks
5. b. The Interstate Slayer
6. Vampire
7. d. 250–450
8. True
9. Because he was believed to have stopped killing for more than a decade.
10. a. Mothers

Eyewitness Testimony

emit
emits
entity
item
items
mint
mints
mist
misty
mite
mites
mitten
mittens
moisten
money
monies
most
noise
noisy
note
notes
omen
omens
omit
omits
set
smitten
soy
stent
stint
stone
ten
tens
tent
tents
test
time
times
tint
tints
tony
totem
totems
toy
toys
yeti

A Night at Raven Manor

Suspect/Alibi/Witness:

art critic/at a restaurant/ boyfriend

security guard/another part of gallery/surveillance cameras

gallery owner/at home/neighbor

artist in residence/different gallery/sign-in sheet

custodian/organizing supplies/ sister on FaceTime

Early Warning Signs of Serial Killers

A	B	C	D	E	F	G	H	I	J	K	L	M
4	1	17	2	19	9	8	5	24	22	26	10	7

N	O	P	Q	R	S	T	U	V	W	X	Y	Z
15	14	12	23	3	6	18	25	21	13	16	11	20

1. ANTISOCIAL BEHAVIOR
2. ARSON
3. TORTURES SMALL ANIMALS
4. POOR FAMILY LIFE
5. CHILDHOOD ABUSE
6. SUBSTANCE ABUSE
7. VOYEURISM
8. INTELLIGENCE
9. SHIFTLESSNESS

Sudoku #3

3	5	6	7	1	2	8	4	9
2	9	8	6	3	4	1	5	7
1	7	4	5	9	8	6	3	2
7	2	3	9	5	6	4	1	8
4	6	5	8	7	1	2	9	3
8	1	9	2	4	3	7	6	5
9	4	2	3	6	7	5	8	1
6	3	7	1	8	5	9	2	4
5	8	1	4	2	9	3	7	6

Female Serial Killers

1. c. She was captured after a minor traffic accident in one of her victims' cars.
2. False. It was because she murdered between 42 and 48 elderly women.
3. Nurse
4. a. Arsenic
5. c. Killer Grandma
6. True
7. c. An anthropology course
8. True
9. b. Precognitive dreams
10. Juice

Magic Square #3

4	9	2
3	5	7
8	1	6

Magic Square #4

6	7	2
1	5	9
8	3	4

Fingerprint Match

Suspect 3

Loan Sharks, Gamblers, and Bootleggers—Oh My!

1. d. Luciano
2. La Cosa Nostra
3. a. Omertà
4. b. Sicily
5. True
6. d. 300 years
7. c. Luxor
8. Fronting
9. True
10. a. Cover themselves in elaborate, complex tattoos

Spot the Fake

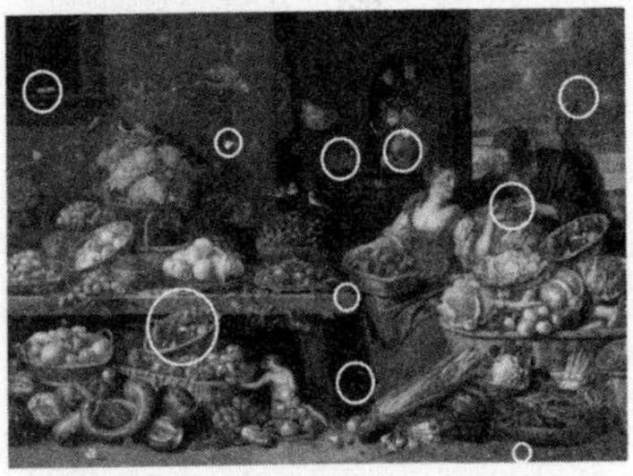

A Bad Investment

Across

3. BLESSINGS
7. BANK
8. BASEBALL
10. CHEAP
11. PETER
14. ABOVE
15. INVESTMENT
20. RETURN
21. EVENT
22. BERNIE MADOFF
24. ROARS
26. TOP
27. OFFSHORE

Down

1. CHARLES PONZI
2. RISK

4. SWINDLE
5. INVESTOR
6. WALL STREET
9. HEDGE FUND
10. CREATE
12. NEWER
13. DONATE
15. INNS
16. PROFIT
17. SEC
18. GENERATOR
19. DOE
22. BILK
23. ASSETS
25. MONEY

Futoshiki #3

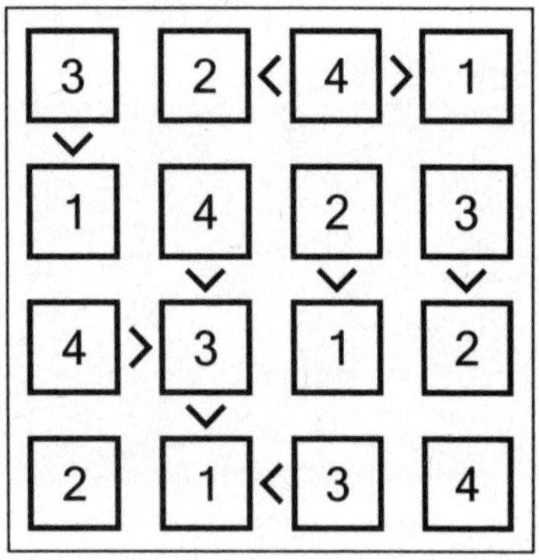

Futoshiki #4

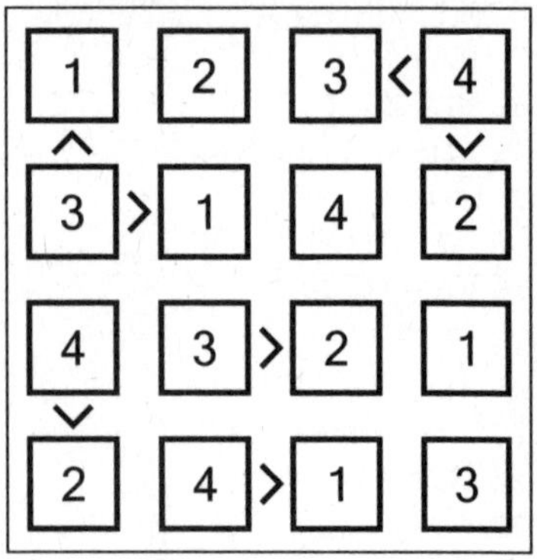

In the Valley of Ice and Death

1. Island
2. Sabotage
3. DNA
4. Address
5. Lindbergh
6. Wire fraud
7. Oath
8. Malpractice
9. Acrobat
10. Negative

Answer: Isdal Woman

Sudoku #4

4	2	1	9	6	8	3	5	7
3	5	6	2	1	7	8	4	9
9	7	8	5	4	3	2	6	1
5	8	7	3	2	6	1	9	4
2	9	4	1	7	5	6	8	3
6	1	3	8	9	4	7	2	5
1	6	9	4	3	2	5	7	8
7	3	5	6	8	9	4	1	2
8	4	2	7	5	1	9	3	6

Land, Ho!

1. b. Straits of Malacca and Singapore
2. True
3. d. All of the above
4. Banana
5. a. Project Compass
6. c. Using nets instead of poles
7. High
8. False. It extends up to 12 nautical miles.
9. b. United States
10. d. My Pirate

Kakuro #2

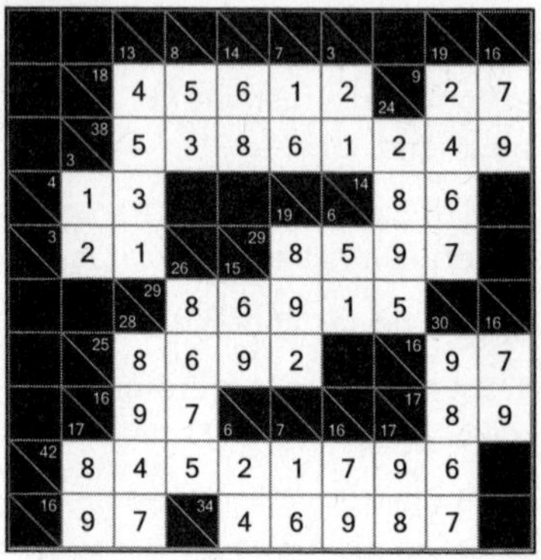

Forensics

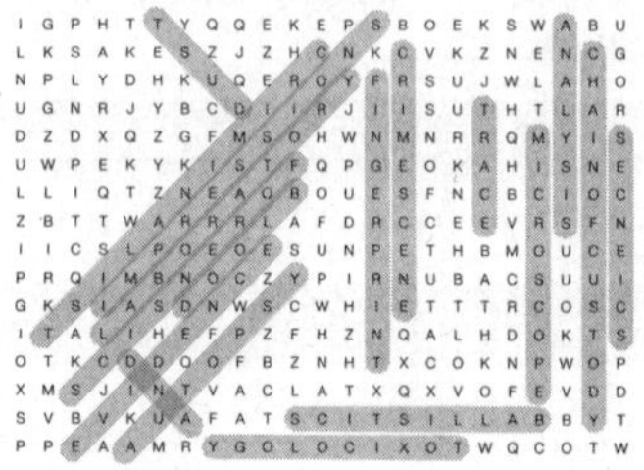

Breakout

1. a. Parole
2. True
3. The Rock
4. b. Reading
5. c. Eighth Amendment
6. False. There are more jails than colleges.
7. a. A hijacked helicopter
8. d. Lack of employment options
9. Recidivism
10. b. Tree nursery

Forged Passport

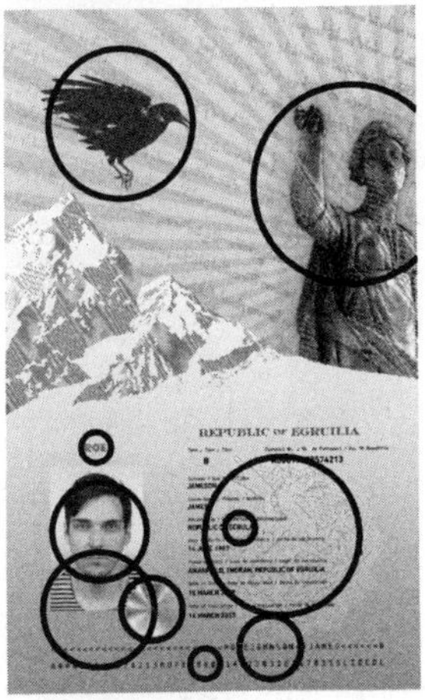

Texas Rangers

1. Austin
2. frontier
3. prairie patrolmen
4. scandal
5. cattle rustler
6. militia
7. protection
8. Plum Creek

Notable Criminals

1. c. Cocaine
2. True
3. a. Because he owed King $600.
4. Varsity Blues
5. True
6. b. Paris
7. Valentine's Day
8. b. Nicole Richie
9. a. A guitar
10. Winona Ryder

Sudoku #5

7	9	3	4	6	1	8	5	2
2	4	8	9	5	3	1	6	7
1	5	6	7	8	2	4	9	3
6	8	7	1	9	4	2	3	5
3	2	5	6	7	8	9	4	1
9	1	4	2	3	5	6	7	8
8	6	9	3	1	7	5	2	4
5	7	2	8	4	6	3	1	9
4	3	1	5	2	9	7	8	6

Evidence Board

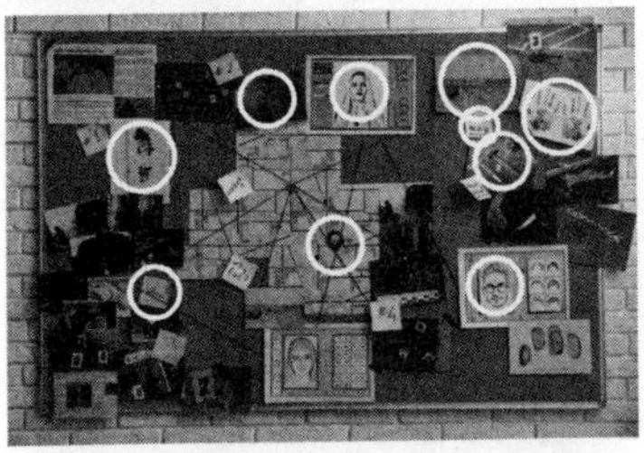

Letter from the Circleville, Ohio, Mystery Writer

A	B	C	D	E	F	G	H	I	J	K	L	M
6	18	10	22	26	19	24	13	9	1	3	25	16

N	O	P	Q	R	S	T	U	V	W	X	Y	Z
20	2	11	12	21	23	7	4	5	17	15	14	8

MRS. GILLISPIE: STAY AWAY FROM MASSIE: DON'T LIE WHEN QUESTIONED ABOUT MEETING HIM. I KNOW WHERE YOU LIVE: I'VE BEEN OBSERVING YOUR HOUSE AND KNOW YOU HAVE CHILDREN. THIS IS NO JOKE. PLEASE TAKE IT SERIOUS. EVERYONE CONCERNED HAS BEEN NOTIFIED. IT WILL BE OVER SOON

Criminal Justice

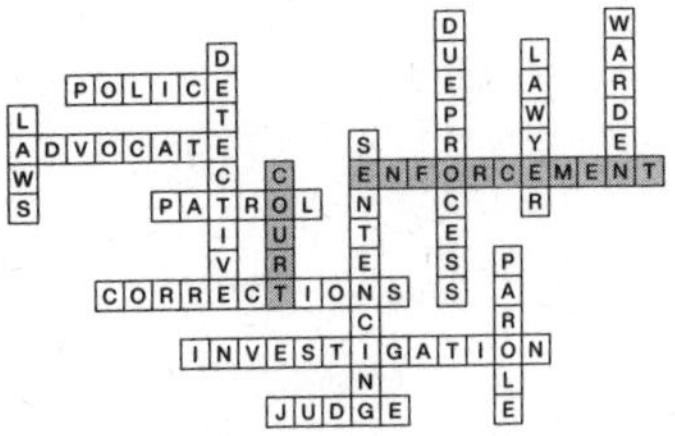

Magic Square #5

6	1	8
7	5	3
2	9	4

Magic Square #6

8	3	4
1	5	9
6	7	2

Bizarre Crimes

1. True
2. a. Marijuana
3. b. Krispy Kreme doughnuts
4. c. Teenage boy
5. Therapist
6. True
7. b. The world's largest commercially available fondue set
8. d. The pizzeria incorrectly put cheese on her garlic knots.
9. b. He applied for a job at the store.

H. H. Holmes's Murder Castle

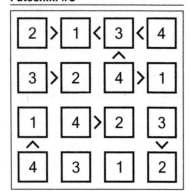

Futoshiki #5

```
2 > 1 < 3 < 4
        ^
3 > 2   4 > 1

1   4 > 2   3
^           v
4   3   1   2
```

Futoshiki #6

```
4 > 1   3 > 2

2   3   1 < 4
        ^
3 < 4   2   1

1   2   4 > 3
```

All Rise

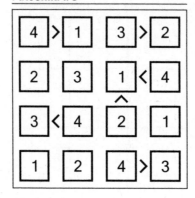

1. a. Habeas corpus
2. Prosecutor
3. False. The defendant chooses.
4. b. During jury selection
5. c. Dissenting
6. True
7. d. Local
8. Indictment
9. c. Parties
10. Motion

Forensic Investigations 101

Analyst/Area of Expertise/Case:

Lana/DNA analysis/triple homicide

Paul/ballistics/drive-by shooting

Ryan/toxicology/car accident

Kristin/chromatography/drug bust

Manish/impression analysis/missing persons

Exhibit A

cede
deceive
den
devein
device
dice
die
din
dine
dive
eden
end
endive
envied
eve
even
evened
evince
evinced
ice
iced
need
nice
niece
vein
veined
vice
vie
vied
vine
vined

Sudoku #6

4	5	1	3	6	2	9	8	7
7	2	8	4	9	1	6	5	3
6	3	9	8	5	7	4	2	1
8	9	3	2	1	6	7	4	5
1	6	7	5	4	9	2	3	8
5	4	2	7	8	3	1	6	9
9	8	5	6	7	4	3	1	2
3	7	6	1	2	8	5	9	4
2	1	4	9	3	5	8	7	6

Tunneling for Reais

1. Flee
2. Overseas
3. Rikers Island
4. Teamsters
5. Always
6. Lawsuit
7. Exonerate
8. Zeal
9. Arrested

Answer: Fortaleza

Kakuro #3

17	9	7	13		38	17
29 / 39	9	8	5	7	15 / 22	6	9
41	9	5	1	2	6	7	3	8
10 / 8	7	3		15 / 18 / 12	6	9
7	6	1	30 / 14	6	7	9	8	15
5	2	3	20 / 17	8	7	5	19	4	6
28	8	9	6	5		14 / 16	5	9
11 / 10	5	6	12 / 6	15	11	9	2
39	9	4	2	7	5	8	3	1
3	1	2	17	5	1	7	4

Unsolved Mysteries

1. c. Dyatlov Pass incident
2. True
3. a. Buried beef liver in the rubble and passed it off as a human heart
4. A pair of dark wraparound sunglasses
5. False. The Axeman never used his own tools and only used what he could find in the victim's house, which was usually an axe.
6. b. A human arm
7. True
8. d. Lines
9. Shark
10. Leatherman

DNA Sequence

Suspect 11

Cults

Across
4. BALLET
5. MANIPULATE
7. GURU
8. DOOMSDAY
10. SEER
14. COMPOUND
17. JOAQUIN
18. MITTENS
20. TOWER
21. UFO
22. EXPLOIT
24. HALF
26. TOKYO
27. FREE
28. GAME
29. HOLIDAY

Down
1. BARCODES
2. CHARISMA
3. ZEALOUS
6. FOLLOWER
9. JESUS CHRIST
11. CUB
12. CONTROL
13. ANNEX
15. PJS
16. DOCTRINE
19. ISOLATED
23. NOG
25. FEET
27. FLOWER

Magic Square #7

2	9	4
7	5	3
6	1	8

Magic Square #8

2	7	6
9	5	1
4	3	8

True Crime Media

1. d. Consuming true crime makes people less empathetic.
2. True
3. b. *Under the Porch*
4. False. It's one in three Americans.
5. *Unsolved Mysteries*
6. a. The Radlett murder
7. b. *Dahmer—Monster: The Jeffrey Dahmer Story*
8. Hae Min Lee
9. c. Jack the Ripper
10. True

Types of Crime

R	Z	V	I	M	S	S	M	R	H	L	G	T	D	O	N	N	K	N	T	H	C	T
B	C	L	X	L	F	O	X	Y	W	K	S	K	J	F	R	A	U	D	V	E	P	X
N	P	U	R	A	R	S	O	N	I	G	P	H	Y	O	K	B	W	T	E	H	T	Q
H	Y	O	N	V	V	A	N	D	A	L	I	S	M	Z	O	B	F	F	I	A	V	O
O	H	L	X	L	T	A	N	N	Q	Q	C	U	Q	J	N	E	T	S	X	U	L	W
M	P	A	C	Q	K	A	P	C	Q	G	X	H	O	U	H	R	H	E	M	N	V	V
I	Z	R	E	Q	P	T	O	B	J	T	A	P	R	T	A	I	V	F	V	M	Z	T
C	V	C	S	P	U	Q	R	W	C	C	U	D	Y	F	N	A	L	B	D	Q	L	F
I	M	E	I	E	I	I	P	Q	K	P	N	T	F	G	S	X	I	J	L	E	J	O
D	V	N	E	L	B	A	K	I	J	A	I	I	K	I	R	F	D	X	L	M	I	Y
E	G	Y	B	E	P	U	N	C	T	T	C	A	O	O	U	T	L	U	A	S	S	A
L	L	C	R	H	P	G	W	I	N	K	J	N	B	Q	T	S	C	A	M	S	H	L
O	U	Y	M	E	M	B	H	E	I	E	M	B	E	Z	Z	L	E	M	E	N	T	V
R	P	P	S	L	Y	G	D	N	V	X	E	N	V	V	F	V	Q	V	R	P	D	B
F	U	Y	Y	K	U	I	G	O	G	R	I	B	V	D	H	J	J	P	E	C	H	P
Y	C	N	A	U	R	T	E	W	Y	M	V	S	E	A	I	S	T	B	A	D	J	I

Sudoku #7

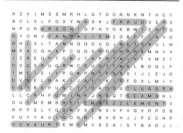

4	9	2	8	5	3	1	7	6
5	6	1	7	9	2	4	3	8
8	7	3	1	4	6	9	5	2
2	8	6	3	1	4	7	9	5
3	1	9	6	7	5	8	2	4
7	5	4	9	2	8	3	6	1
9	2	5	4	3	1	6	8	7
6	4	7	5	8	9	2	1	3
1	3	8	2	6	7	5	4	9

Blackmail Letter from the "Monster with 21 Faces"

A	B	C	D	E	F	G	H	I	J	K	L	M
5	16	22	4	9	19	2	6	25	13	21	11	24

N	O	P	Q	R	S	T	U	V	W	X	Y	Z
10	18	12	26	1	20	23	7	15	3	17	8	14

DEAR STUPID POLICE OFFICERS. DON'T LIE. ALL CRIMES BEGIN WITH A LIE AS WE SAY IN JAPAN. DON'T YOU KNOW THAT? YOU SEEM TO BE AT A LOSS.

Surveillance Camera Footage

Under Attack

1. a. Denmark
2. True
3. d. Illegal drug trade
4. Email
5. b. Computer intrusion squad
6. False. Human error accounts for 95 percent of security breaches.
7. c. Keystroke
8. a. Robert's friend spoke to a reporter and inadvertently referred to him by his initials.
9. c. Corporate
10. Phishing

Kakuro #4

■	■	33\	4\	15\	■	15\	17\	■	■
■	13\16	4	3	9	38\16	7	9	■	■
\33	4	9	1	6	3	2	8	36\	16\
\17	9	8	8\	16\15	9	6	\8	1	7
■	\25	6	3	9	7	4\	12\15	6	9
■	7\36	2	5	7	8	1	4	9	■
\3	2	1	■	18\24	6	3	8	7	9\
\8	5	3	6\13	9	4	14\	7\3	2	1
■	■	\35	2	7	1	9	5	3	8
■	■	\6	4	2	\15	5	2	8	■

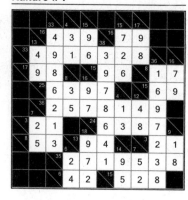

A Priceless Treasure

1. Mobster
2. Ole
3. Noir
4. Alias
5. Lake
6. Imposter
7. Suspect
8. Author

Answer: Mona Lisa

Coroner vs. Medical Examiner

1. Crown
2. a. Suffolk County, Massachusetts
3. True
4. False. Coroners are not required to have formal medical or forensic training, and only 16 states have laws with specific training requirements.
5. d. All of the above
6. False. Coroners are elected officials, while medical examiners are specially appointed physicians who report to medical organizations.
7. b. Surgical incision
8. Inquest or inquisition
9. c. France and Scotland
10. a. New York City

Sticky Fingers

Sudoku #8

2	3	8	6	4	1	5	9	7
7	4	6	3	5	9	2	8	1
5	1	9	8	7	2	6	4	3
3	6	7	2	8	4	9	1	5
8	2	1	9	6	5	3	7	4
4	9	5	7	1	3	8	6	2
1	5	2	4	9	8	7	3	6
9	7	4	5	3	6	1	2	8
6	8	3	1	2	7	4	5	9

The Great Train Robbery

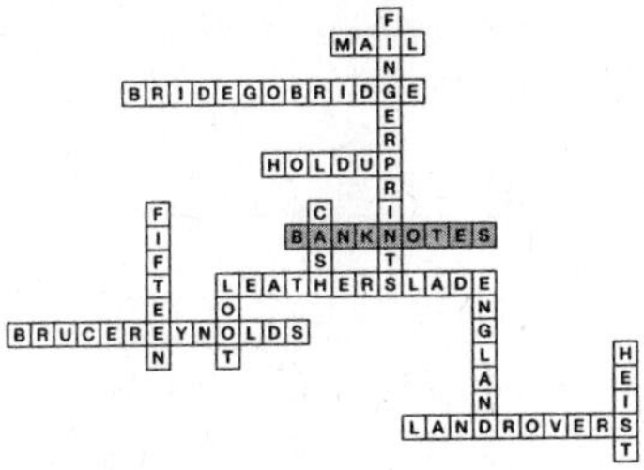

Cecil Hotel

1. macabre
2. murder
3. Skid Row
4. Night Stalker
5. violence
6. Black Dahlia
7. bizarre
8. Pigeon Lady

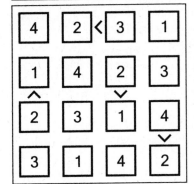

Futoshiki #7

4	2 <	3	1
1	4	2	3
^		v	
2	3	1	4
			v
3	1	4	2

Futoshiki #8

2	4	3	1
v			
1	3 <	4	2
3	2	1	4
^			
4	1	2	3

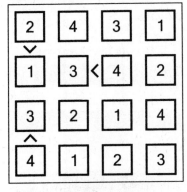

True Crime and Pop Culture

1. d. *Child's Play*'s Charles Lee Ray
2. True
3. *The Lone Ranger*
4. a. *Final Fantasy VII*
5. c. Jeffrey Dahmer
6. b. *White Album*
7. True
8. c. "Don't go upstairs."
9. *The Catcher in the Rye*
10. False; it's about the Boston Strangler.

Seized Jewelry

Magic Square #9

2	15	14	3
11	10	7	6
5	8	9	12
16	1	4	13

Magic Square #10

3	13	6	12
9	16	7	2
8	1	10	15
14	4	11	5

'70s Crime

1. Tried to assassinate President Gerald Ford
2. False. Cousins Angelo Buono Jr. and Kenneth Bianchi pled guilty to the crimes and were sentenced to life in prison.
3. The Symbionese Liberation Army kidnapped her.
4. A camera tripod
5. False. He was known for luring his victims by flattering them with quick sketches of them.
6. c. He's in the witness protection program.
7. a. It's theorized that the young pilot Frederick Valentich was captured by a UFO.
8. Car bombs
9. b. Copious amounts of blood on the walls of the basement of the killer's father's home

Gentleman of the Road

again	main	wig
am	man	win
any	manga	wing
away	mangy	yam
gain	mania	yawn
gin	many	
gnaw	may	
gym	my	
hag	nag	
ham	nigh	
hang	wag	
hay	wan	
hi	way	
high	wham	
highway	whig	
him	whim	
hymn	whiny	
in	why	

Heist Mix-Up

Heist/Location/Stolen Item/Year

Brink's-Mat Warehouse heist/London/gold bars/1983

Antwerp Vault heist/Belgium/diamonds/2003

Isabella Stewart Gardner Museum theft/Boston/works of art/1994

Banco Central burglary/Fortaleza/cash/2005

The Strängnäs Cathedral heist/Sweden/royal jewels/2018

D. B. Cooper Hijacking Note

A	B	C	D	E	F	G	H	I	J	K	L	M
10	19	21	1	22	14	23	25	16	2	24	6	26

N	O	P	Q	R	S	T	U	V	W	X	Y	Z
11	15	17	7	13	8	20	3	5	9	4	12	18

I WANT $200,000 BY 5 P.M. IN CASH EXCLUSIVELY IN $20 BILLS, PUT IN A KNAPSACK. I WANT TWO BACK PARACHUTES AND TWO FRONT PARACHUTES. WHEN WE LAND, I WANT A FUEL TRUCK READY TO REFUEL. NO FUNNY STUFF OR I'LL DO THE JOB.

Sudoku #9

5	1	9	6	3	4	2	7	8
6	8	3	2	7	9	5	4	1
4	2	7	5	1	8	9	3	6
8	3	4	9	5	6	1	2	7
7	6	5	1	2	3	4	8	9
1	9	2	8	4	7	6	5	3
2	7	1	3	9	5	8	6	4
3	5	8	4	6	1	7	9	2
9	4	6	7	8	2	3	1	5

Do You Swear to Tell the Truth?

2

Political Crimes

1. Bribery
2. Influence
3. d. All of the above
4. True
5. a. Because he had not overtly done anything, only planned it.
6. True
7. b. Tennessee Waltz
8. False. It was the Teapot Dome Scandal of the 1920s.
9. b. Sedition
10. c. Costa Rica

Labyrinth of Lies

Types of Evidence

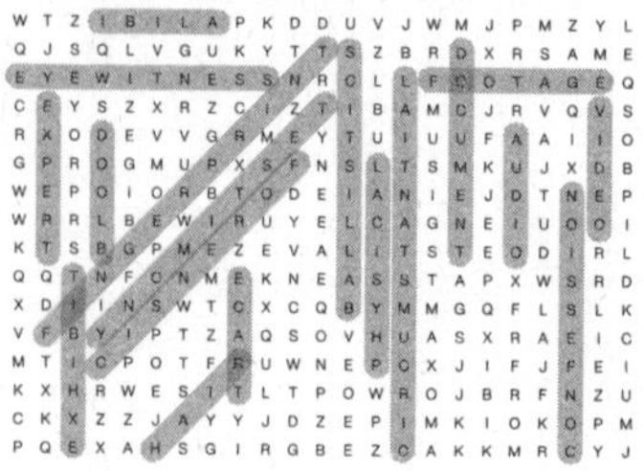

'80s Crime

1. The jury found that DeLorean had been a victim of government entrapment.
2. b. He shot his would-be muggers, four teenagers who blocked his exit from the number 2 train, and demanded $5.
3. True
4. Ozzy Osbourne
5. True
6. c. Genetic genealogy
7. d. All of the above
8. John Gotti
9. The Chippendales

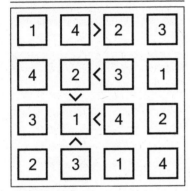

Futoshiki #9

1		4	>	2		3
4		2	<	3		1
		∨				
3		1	<	4		2
		∧				
2		3		1		4

Futoshiki #10

4	>	2	<	3		1
∨		∧				
1		3		2	<	4
3		4		1		2
2		1	<	4	>	3

Kakuro #5

	17\	23\				16\	15\	34\	
\15	9	6	7\	14\	\22	9	6	7	23\
\20	8	9	1	2	17\26	7	9	4	6
	\20	8	6	5	1		6\14	6	8
		24\	16\3	1	2	16\21	4	8	9
	23\39	8	7	6	3	4	2	9	
\23	8	6	9	\11	5	6	10\	23\	
\7	6	1	14\	17\19	6	1	3	9	17\
\28	9	5	6	8	\29	5	7	8	9
	\21	4	8	9			\14	6	8

Criminal Profiling

Across

3. VICTIM
8. MONTANA
9. ANALYSIS
11. VICAP
13. VICTIMOLOGY
14. DATABASE
17. DOUGLAS
20. SIGNATURE
21. PERSONALITY
22. EVIDENCE
25. MODUS OPERANDI
26. ERROR
28. ABILITY
30. TRACKER

Down

1. FBI
2. DIRTY DOZEN
4. CRIME SCENE
5. PATTERNS
6. TARGETED
7. REVERSE ENGINEER
10. HOKUM
12. PSYCHOLOGY
15. TED BUNDY
16. LAPSE
18. SERIAL
19. MAD BOMBER
23. BEHAVIORAL
24. UNSUB
27. NARROW
29. THEORY

Rogues' Gallery

1. Mole
2. Undercover
3. Gamble
4. Smuggle
5. Hijack
6. Orange
7. Tennis

Answer: Mug Shot

Sudoku #10

1	4	8	3	9	2	5	7	6
7	5	2	4	6	8	9	1	3
9	3	6	5	7	1	8	4	2
8	7	4	9	2	3	6	5	1
5	9	1	7	4	6	3	2	8
6	2	3	8	1	5	7	9	4
2	8	7	1	3	9	4	6	5
4	6	5	2	8	7	1	3	9
3	1	9	6	5	4	2	8	7

Criminal Investigative Analysis

1. Step 1: Profiling inputs, Step 2: Constructing a Decision Process Model, Step 3: Crime Assessment, Step 4: Criminal Profile, Step 5: Investigation, Step 6: Apprehension
2. a. Metropolitan Police surgeon Thomas Bond's report about Jack the Ripper
3. c. John Douglas
4. d. 1984
5. a. JonBenet Ramsey
6. b. Classifying serial homicide crime scenes according to an organized/disorganized dichotomy.
7. True
8. c. Drove a pickup truck
9. c. 36

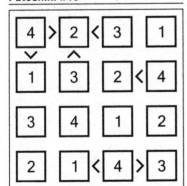

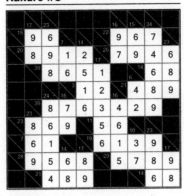

Magic Square #11

6	10	7	11
3	15	2	14
9	5	12	8
16	4	13	1

Magic Square #12

9	6	12	7
5	10	8	11
4	3	13	14
16	15	1	2

Undercover Investigations

Anna "Delvey" Sorokin

1. con artist
2. fake heiress
3. defraud
4. scammer
5. falsify
6. socialite
7. arts club
8. Rikers Island

'90s Crime

1. a. Axl Rose
2. b. Scott revealed he had a crush on Jonathan.
3. False. It was her fan club president and friend.
4. c. 1996 Atlanta, Georgia, summer games
5. True
6. d. Gun control laws
7. Amy Fisher, who shot her boyfriend's wife
8. a. The acquittal of LAPD officers after their use of excessive force to arrest Rodney King.
9. c. Phil Hartman

Shoe Prints

7

Sudoku #11

7	6	8	5	2	9	3	4	1
5	4	9	8	3	1	2	6	7
2	1	3	4	6	7	5	8	9
8	9	1	6	5	4	7	2	3
6	5	2	3	7	8	9	1	4
4	3	7	1	9	2	6	5	8
1	2	5	9	8	3	4	7	6
3	7	4	2	1	6	8	9	5
9	8	6	7	4	5	1	3	2

A Dead End

Ransom Letter from Adolph Coors III's Kidnapper

A	B	C	D	E	F	G	H	I	J	K	L	M
23	6	13	4	2	10	8	11	1	3	22	20	7

N	O	P	Q	R	S	T	U	V	W	X	Y	Z
16	9	21	17	18	19	12	14	24	26	5	15	25

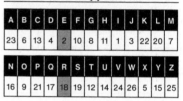

MRS. COORS: YOUR HUSBAND HAS BEEN KIDNAPPED. HIS CAR IS BY TURKEY CREEK. CALL THE POLICE OR F.B.I.: HE DIES. COOPERATE: HE LIVES. RANSOM: $200,000 IN TENS AND $300,000 IN TWENTIES. THERE WILL BE NO NEGOTIATING. BILLS: USED/NON-CONSECUTIVE/UNRECORDED/UNMARKED. WARNING: WE WILL KNOW IF YOU CALL THE POLICE OR RECORD THE SERIAL NUMBERS.

Spill the Beans

1. Innocent
2. Noble
3. Felony
4. Omission
5. Racketeering
6. Memory
7. Accessory
8. Night
9. Tickle the wire

Answer: Informant

'00s Crime

1. Bernie Madoff
2. a. Portugal
3. c. Enron
4. b. A tarot "Death" card
5. True
6. Martha Stewart
7. Breathing or lungs
8. b. Video recordings of him torturing his victims
9. b. Baton Rouge
10. True

Tracking a Killer

Pay the Piper

emit
emits
ennui
he
heist
hem
hemp
hems
hen
hens
him
hint
hip
his
hit
hitmen
hits
hue
hues
hum
hump
hunt
huntsmen
hut
impetus
inn
inns
input
inset
instep
item
its
menu
mine
mines
mint
mints
minuet
minus
minute
minutes
mist
mite
muse
mush
must
mut
mute
mutes
nest
nine
nines
ninth
nip
nips
nun
nuns
nut
nuts
pest
pet
pets
pie
pies
pin
pine
pins
pines
pint
pints
pit
pits
pun
punish
pus
push
puts
semi
sent
septum
set
she
shine
shipment
shun
shunt
sin
smith
smut
snip
snipe
spent
spine
spit
stein
stem
step
stump
suit
suite
sum
sun
supine
temp
ten
tennis
the
then
thin
thins
this
thus
tie
ties
time
times
tin
tine
tins
tines
tip
tips
unit
unite
units
unites
unpin
unpins
unsent
up

Home, Sweet—Oh!

1. b. An axe
2. a. High Hopes
3. d. Set the house on fire
4. True
5. d. The neighbors in his apartment building complained of blocked drains—which were caused by human remains.
6. c. *Clueless*
7. True
8. A safe
9. False. She was acquitted; also they were killed with a hatchet-like weapon.

Kakuro #6

	22\	43\		13\	5\	8\	6\		
\9	5	4	\13	6	4	2	1	37\	20\
\16	9	7	\25	7	1	6	5	2	4
\13	8	5	15\		17\	14\	\16	7	9
	\16	9	7	7\13	8	5	13\12	5	7
	21\38	3	8	2	7	9	5	4	
\6	5	1	\7	5	2	\17	8	9	20\
\17	9	8	16\	9\	10\	17\	\12	3	9
\39	7	6	9	5	4	8	\10	6	4
		\26	7	4	6	9	\8	1	7

Cold Cases Cracked

Moniker/Location/Victim/Year

Lady of the Dunes/Provincetown, MA/Ruth Marie Terry/1974

Bear Brook murders/New Hampshire/Marlyse Elizabeth Honeychurch/1985

Somerton Man/Australia/Carl "Charles" Webb/1948

Boy in the Box/Philadelphia/Joseph Augustus Zarelli/1957

Little Miss Nobody/Arizona/Sharon Lee Gallegos/1960

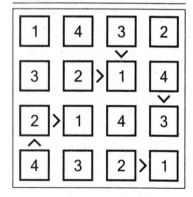

Sudoku #12

3	5	8	4	7	2	9	6	1
2	4	7	1	6	9	3	5	8
6	1	9	3	5	8	4	7	2
7	2	3	5	8	4	6	1	9
5	9	1	2	3	6	8	4	7
8	6	4	9	1	7	5	2	3
9	3	5	6	2	1	7	8	4
4	8	2	7	9	5	1	3	6
1	7	6	8	4	3	2	9	5

Futoshiki #11

1		4		3		2
				∨		
3		2	>	1		4
						∨
2	>	1		4		3
∧						
4		3		2	>	1

Futoshiki #12

4		1	<	3		2
∨						
2		3		1		4
		∨				
1		2		4	>	3
∧						∨
3	<	4		2		1

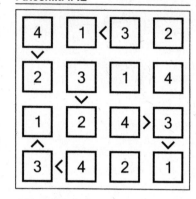

All or Nothing

1. True
2. b. Card counting
3. An armored vehicle
4. False. Scotland Yard determined no crime had been committed, and they were able to keep their winnings.
5. a. At least ten employees saw his face.
6. Because he wore a full-face motorcycle helmet and escaped on a motorcycle.
7. True. Even though Bill was on the FBI's Most Wanted list, the case was dropped in 2006 when the casino shut down.
8. Third
9. b. He posed as the owner of the casino and convinced a hotel employee to send him the money.
10. a. A casino boss ordered her to bring the cash to an attorney in a hospital parking lot.

Black Sox Scandal

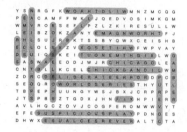

Y	S	N	R	G	F	K	W	O	R	H	T	D	L	I	W	M	N	Z	M	C	Q	G
P	E	A	C	A	M	F	F	W	K	L	J	Q	E	D	V	O	S	I	M	K	G	M
W	M	V	R	O	E	S	E	F	L	P	Z	L	Z	K	I	R	E	S	U	L	L	W
L	E	I	B	Z	O	K	Z	A	N	Y	E	M	A	G	N	W	O	R	H	T	F	J
R	H	L	S	U	J	R	B	K	T	S	S	B	Y	Q	W	X	C	E	I	S	H	B
E	C	L	O	L	S	E	Z	V	X	O	S	E	T	I	H	W	F	W	P	V	A	Y
D	S	U	I	Q	S	K	E	I	T	U	O	N	E	M	T	H	G	I	E	L	W	G
S	A	S	W	A	E	E	O	D	J	W	J	R	C	H	I	C	A	G	O	L	E	A
C	N	T	B	L	L	K	C	E	L	C	H	I	C	K	G	A	N	D	I	L	W	M
Z	D	R	C	D	E	L	I	B	E	R	A	T	E	E	R	R	O	R	D	P	C	B
S	E	O	Q	R	O	W	O	R	L	D	S	E	R	I	E	S	T	H	Y	U	T	L
T	B	P	E	P	H	U	U	N	G	Y	W	S	J	B	X	J	C	R	P	R	P	E
J	T	S	P	B	S	Z	T	G	D	X	J	H	N	F	I	X	H	P	I	E	R	R
A	V	L	H	Q	C	Z	O	V	J	C	O	G	F	E	R	O	M	W	W	V	Y	T
E	F	E	S	U	S	P	I	C	I	O	U	S	P	L	A	Y	P	D	N	O	E	S
D	H	W	X	E	S	U	A	L	C	E	S	R	E	V	E	R	A	L	T	C	T	A

Magic Square #13

10	45	20
35	25	15
30	5	40

Magic Square #14

6	27	12
21	15	9
18	3	24

Crime Lab

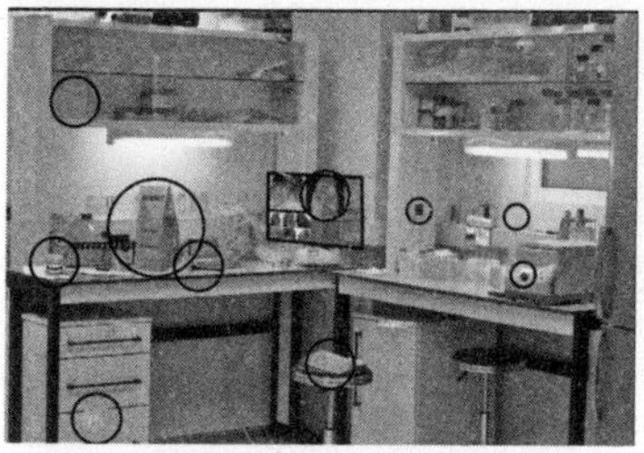

"You and I Are Going to Make a Lot of Money Together"

1. a. 1849
2. c. He gained people's trust quickly and convinced them to hand over their watches.
3. Psychic
4. b. A spy
5. True
6. c. Stanley Kubrick
7. b. A TV producer
8. a. Narcissism, b. Psychopathy, d. Machiavellianism
9. False. Con artists play to emotions.
10. Confidence man

Sudoku #13

3	9	6	1	8	2	7	5	4
8	5	7	9	4	6	3	2	1
4	2	1	3	5	7	9	8	6
5	4	3	7	9	1	8	6	2
9	1	2	8	6	5	4	3	7
6	7	8	4	2	3	1	9	5
2	8	9	5	7	4	6	1	3
7	3	5	6	1	9	2	4	8
1	6	4	2	3	8	5	7	9

Alcatraz Escapee's Letter

A	B	C	D	E	F	G	H	I	J	K	L	M
23	10	19	18	8	6	26	12	20	11	13	16	7

N	O	P	Q	R	S	T	U	V	W	X	Y	Z
21	3	15	22	25	4	17	1	14	5	24	2	9

MY NAME IS JOHN ANGLIN. I ESCAPED FROM ALCATRAZ IN JUNE 1962 WITH MY BROTHER CLARENCE AND FRANK MORRIS. I'M 83 YEARS OLD AND IN BAD SHAPE. I HAVE CANCER. YES WE ALL MADE IT THAT NIGHT BUT BARELY! IF YOU ANNOUNCE ON TV THAT I WILL BE PROMISED TO FIRST GO TO JAIL FOR NO MORE THAN A YEAR AND GET MEDICAL ATTENTION, I WILL WRITE BACK TO LET YOU KNOW EXACTLY WHERE I AM. THIS IS NO JOKE.

Cybercrime

Across

3. SOCIAL
7. EBOOK
8. SONY
9. OREO
11. VPN
13. PHISHING
15. BREACH
17. BRUSQUE
19. DARK WEB
21. CATFISHING
24. SPEAR
25. MALWARE
26. ODOR
28. MORRIS
29. ERE
30. BEC

Down

1. ESPIONAGE
2. FACTOR
4. ZERO
5. SERVICE
6. NOUN
10. ENCRYPT
12. FIREWALL
14. ASHLEY
16. IDENTITY
18. HACKER
20. RANSOMWARE
22. SPOOFING
23. PASSWORD
27. EMU

Tire Tracks Match

2

Covert Actions

1. False. A spy is either a volunteer or recruit used to steal secrets for an intelligence organization.
2. Double agent
3. a. Planning, Collection, Processing, Analysis, Dissemination
4. c. The act of spying, usually through illegal means
5. b. Cambridge University
6. True
7. CIA
8. d. German
9. Economic or corporate
10. a. Hilton

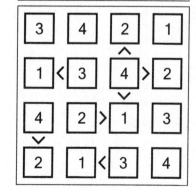

Futoshiki #13

3		4		2		1
				∧		
1	<	3		4	>	2
				∨		
4		2	>	1		3
∨						
2		1	<	3		4

Futoshiki #14

3	1	4	2
2	3	1	4
1	4	2	3
4	2	3	1

Stanford Prison Experiment

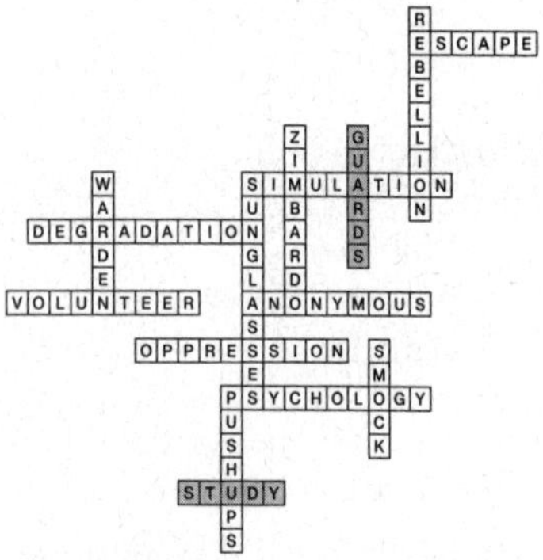

Billy the Kid

1. outlaw
2. orphan
3. gunslinger
4. The Regulators
5. cattle rustler
6. jailbreak
7. Old West
8. Fort Sumner

Cops + Custody + Interrogation

1. Mayhem
2. Ivy
3. Reason
4. Appeal
5. Narcotics
6. Drag
7. Acquittal
8. Robbery
9. Island
10. Graffiti
11. Habit
12. Traffic
13. Statutory

Answer: Miranda rights

Sudoku #14

1	9	5	4	3	6	2	7	8
4	3	6	8	7	2	9	1	5
2	8	7	9	5	1	6	4	3
7	1	8	2	4	5	3	6	9
6	4	9	1	8	3	7	5	2
5	2	3	6	9	7	1	8	4
9	5	1	7	2	8	4	3	6
8	7	4	3	6	9	5	2	1
3	6	2	5	1	4	8	9	7

John B. McLemore's Hedge Maze

Is There a (Real) Doctor in the House?

1. Body parts
2. True
3. a. Brains
4. c. Drowning
5. Healthcare serial killers
6. False. She gave the patient a paralytic instead of a sedative.
7. b. Opioids
8. a. Fen-Phen
9. True
10. d. Heath Ledger

ABOUT THE AUTHOR

Lana Barnes can usually be found hunched over a puzzle, whether it's a traditional pen-and-paper one, online, or her favorite, a murder mystery board game. When not absorbed in cracking the latest head-scratcher, Lana loves reading, enjoys traveling with family and friends, and works as a full-time freelance proofreader and children's book reviewer. She lives in central Connecticut with her husband.

Hi there,

We hope you enjoyed *True Crime Trivia & Activity Book*. If you have any questions or concerns about your book, or have received a damaged copy, please contact customerservice@penguinrandomhouse.com. We're here and happy to help.

Also, please consider writing a review on your favorite retailer's website to let others know what you thought of the book!

Sincerely,
The Zeitgeist Team